CHINA AND THE WORLD, 1949–2024

KEN HAMMOND

Published in November 2024 by
1804 Books, New York, NY

1804Books.com

ISBN: 979-8-9910139-2-5
Library of Congress Control Number: 2024946865

Cover by Vivek Venkatraman

TABLE OF CONTENTS

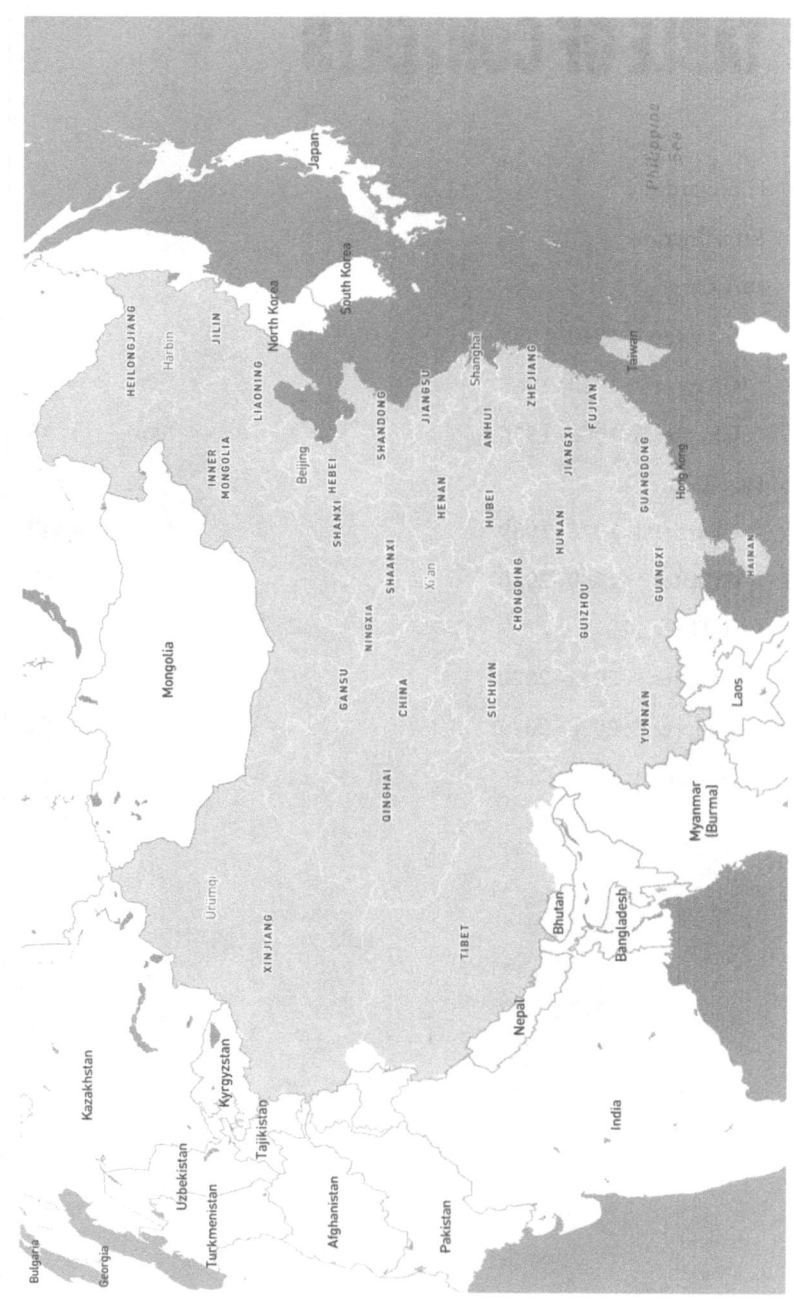

FOREWORD

BRIAN BECKER

The socialist revolution in China was a decades-long epic battle that forever changed China and the world. The Communist Party, led by its chairman Mao Zedong, took the reins of state power in 1949 and charted a new path based on socialist principles. Today, China is the largest economy in the world, and it is also the target of a US-led effort to slow its economic growth and its increasing role as an independent center of economic and political power.

In 2022, I invited Professor Ken Hammond to join *The Socialist Program* podcast for a series of discussions on the stages and phases of China's foreign policy following the communist victory in 1949. We had anticipated the topic would take three shows, each lasting an hour—but we seriously underestimated the endeavor. The series evolved into nine separate shows for eight-and-a-half hours of programming. In addition to appearing as nine separate podcasts, we also decided to reedit and combine all the podcasts into a longer show that encompasses all of the discussions.

Because of the importance of the topic, we decided to publish these nine conversations in book form, but for readability purposes, we decided to change course. Listening to nine hours of discussions between two people is one thing. We felt the verbal discourse worked well as a podcast, but determined that using a more traditional literary approach in book form would be better. Professor Hammond is not only an expert on Chinese history with a keen understanding of the ins and outs of China's politics, but he is also a masterful writer.

This book reflects his views as the interviewee in the nine discussions examining seven-plus decades of China's foreign policy since 1949.

From the beginning of the project, our motivation was to examine China's foreign policy from both a partisan and objective lens. Partisan, in the sense that *The Socialist Program* podcast is a firm supporter of the Chinese Revolution and its socialist aspirations. Objective, however, because we believed that it was necessary for socialists who support the Chinese socialist project to do so using a hard-headed and realistic approach. This view is a necessary antidote to certain political weaknesses that evolved inside of a larger ideological struggle between two distinct trends that have developed since the victory of the socialist revolution in Russia in 1917.

For over a century in countries still under the control of pro-imperialist governments, the socialist movement has been ideologically divided over whether to support or politically defend the socialist governments that have been targeted by imperialism. In general, those socialists who identify with social democracy have joined the pro-imperialist chorus that routinely demonizes the USSR, China, and the other governments led by communist parties. Consciously or unconsciously, this branch of socialism provided a useful service to the imperialist efforts to topple communist-led governments. Having "left" voices join the imperialist choir lent credibility, or at least provided some degree of camouflage, for the predatory character of the anti-communist crusade conducted by the imperialist ruling classes in the US, Europe, and Japan.

A lesser but still important problem came from the camp of socialists who were partisan defenders of the USSR, China, or other socialist governments. While militantly defending these socialist governments, they let go of the need for a strong, politically independent orientation of the problems, difficulties, and contradictions that every communist-led government has encountered. A defense of socialist governments based on an idealist approach suffers from an undeniable problem: such idealism always turns into cynicism when the ideal seems unrealized or unrealizable. The socialist governments are attempting to survive counterrevolution and build socialism, step by step, in an extremely hostile international environment where imperialism and class stratification dominate.

Using the method of historical materialism, in distinction from idealism, Marx wrote: "Men make their own history, but they do not make it as they please; they do not make it under self-selected circumstances, but under circumstances existing already, given and transmitted from the past. The tradition of all dead generations weighs like a nightmare on the brains of the living." The core problem facing the socialist governments of the twentieth century, however, was less the "tradition of all dead generations," as problematic as that is, but, rather, the very still alive camp of global imperialism that has employed military, economic, covert, and diplomatic methods to impede and crush the development of socialism.

The political defense of a socialist government against domestic counterrevolution or imperialist intervention does not require one to become an idealistic cheerleader for the particular foreign policy position of this or that socialist government. Such an orientation has led to great confusion about what it is that must be defended politically in the countries that have socialist governments or governments that are led by a communist party.

Idealism will inevitably turn into its opposite—cynicism and disappointment—due to a failure to understand the implications of a particular reality; that each state, socialist or capitalist, lives within a system of states. The states led by socialist governments are compelled to engage in diplomacy with the capitalist governments that seek to overthrow them through counterrevolution, foreign intervention, or both. Likewise, the economies in countries led by socialist or communist governments are connected by a thousand arteries to the world economy, which must be understood as a global capitalist economy. The rules of the world economy are written by Wall Street bankers and their imperialist colleagues in Western Europe.

China and the World examines China's evolving foreign policy in multiple distinct stages.

The first decade was rooted in the alliance forged between China and the USSR. The new communist government that took power in 1949 was initially incorporated into a larger socialist camp anchored by the Soviet Union. Mao only left China twice during his lifetime—both times to the Soviet Union—but in December 1949, he traveled to Moscow for a series of discussions with Stalin, staying there for two months. In early January 1950, Mao sent a telegram back to the Central Committee of the Chinese Communist Party that read:

> Our work here has achieved an important breakthrough in the past two days. Comrade Stalin has finally agreed to invite Comrade Chou En-lai to Moscow and sign a new Sino-Soviet Treaty of Friendship and Alliance and other agreements on credit, trade, and civil aviation. Yesterday, on January 1, a decision was made to publish my interview with the Tass correspondent, and it is in the newspapers today (January 2), which you might have already received. At 8:00 p.m. today, Comrade Molotov and Comrade Mikoyan came to my quarters to have a talk, asking about my opinions on the Sino-Soviet treaty and other matters. I immediately gave them a detailed description of three options . . . .

China's entrance into the socialist camp was the most defining feature of its foreign policy in the first decade.

The relationship between China and the USSR deteriorated a decade later as the parties leading the two largest socialist countries became engaged in an increasingly bitter ideological struggle, principally rooted in their different orientations toward the United States and the bloc of imperialist nations that were hostile to both the Soviet Union and China. At first, it was a political or ideological struggle, but it devolved over time into a state-to-state dispute.

The 1972 visit of Richard Nixon to meet Mao inaugurated a new phase of China's foreign policy. Within a decade, the US fully normalized its relationship with China and, by the 1980s, embraced China as a friend and strategic partner against the Soviet Union. This was reflected in a new stage of China's foreign policy.

The anti-communist counterrevolution changed the balance of political forces between socialism and capitalism on a global scale, leading to the ousting of communist-led governments in Europe in the late 1980s and eventually to the toppling of the USSR in 1991. Although China had de facto exited—or been expelled—from the bloc of countries that made up the socialist camp by the 1980s, the destruction of the socialist bloc constituted a dire threat to the Chinese government. Starting in 1991, China charted a new foreign policy rooted in the knowledge that the US sought to create a new unipolar world order whereby the United States, and it alone, would be the world's only superpower.

China and the US enjoyed a generally friendly relationship for the last decade of the twentieth century and the first decade of the current one. China had opened up its economy to major investments from US and Western corporations. Chinese students were welcomed into the US and Western universities, and US teachers, researchers and business people were invited to China. During this period, China's foreign policy generally sought to avoid a confrontational position with US policy. There were some exceptions. In 1999, the US Air Force bombed the Chinese Embassy in Belgrade, Yugoslavia during NATO's massive bombing war that destroyed the last communist-led government in Europe. China angrily condemned the bombing and did not accept the US' official explanation that said the bombing of the embassy was a mistake and was not intentional.

China did not support the US invasion of Iraq, or the bombing war waged against Libya in 2011, or the US effort to arm insurgents to topple the government in Syria. But it did little to mount global opposition to these imperialist adventures. In the case of Libya, neither China nor Russia used their veto power to torpedo the US-initiated Resolution 1971 that authorized the use of outside military force against Libya. Roughly speaking, this period of global politics ends in 2014.

World politics has changed dramatically in the last few years and China's new foreign policy reflects those changes. In 2018, the US government adopted a new military doctrine that prioritizes major power conflict as the center of a new Pentagon strategy. The Russian military intervention in Ukraine in 2022 is both a marker and a reflection of that development. The US State Department, Central Intelligence Agency, and much of the mainstream media have also engaged in a multisided campaign against China and Russia during recent years.

Under the leadership of Xi Xinping, the Chinese government's foreign policy seeks to manage the growing conflict with the United States while developing a complex, nuanced strategy for its relations with the countries of the Global South, as well as US allies in Europe and Japan.

The extended interviews with Ken Hammond covered all of these topics. This book reflects a political orientation that is deeply committed to the project of progress in China. It supports the socialist project in a country that is emerging as the most powerful force within the Global South. It examines the shifts, changes, contradictions and evolving priorities of China's foreign policy. Professor Hammond approaches the topic using the method of historical materialism.

China and the World offers a comprehensive survey of China's foreign policy over the past seventy-five years. Readers, especially those who are just exploring the topic for the first time, will find this book to be an invaluable resource to understand China's place in the global politics of the current period.

INTRODUCTION

In 1949, the government of the People's Republic of China had just been instituted—and was met with urgent concerns to address. When the People's Republic of China (PRC) was officially proclaimed by Mao Zedong on October 1, 1949, it had to manage its domestic economic and political issues, as well as grapple with the international context of the Cold War and the long era of imperialist domination which stretched back to the early nineteenth century. From the time of the First Opium War in 1839–1842, through the defeat of the Japanese invasion of 1937–1945, and with the final overthrow of the corrupt regime of the nationalist Guomindang (GMD) in the Civil War of 1945–1949, China had endured repeated humiliations at the hands of the imperialist powers of Europe, the United States, and Japan. With the toppling of the Qing dynasty in 1911–1912 came the collapse of a two-thousand-year-old dynastic system. This opened up an era of political and cultural transformation, but it left much of China in the hands of the ancient landowning elites and the urban commercial class who drove a hybrid capitalist economy based on the exploitation of both manufacturing workers in the cities and a vast population of rural workers on the land.

In the first decades of the twentieth century, many people in China sought new solutions to the deepening crises their country faced. The dual challenges of imperialist domination and domestic oppression fueled a quest for radical change. Some initially hoped to create a liberal republic along the lines of the Western bourgeois democracies, while others began to consider the ideas of socialist and anarchist thinkers and the workers' movements of Europe and North America. The victory of the Bolshevik Revolution in 1917 became an inspiration, followed shortly by the Versailles Peace Conference in 1919, where the Allied powers of World War I betrayed China and handed over former German concessions in Shandong to Japan rather than returning them to Chinese control, exposing the bankruptcy of the liberal rhetoric of self-determination spouted by US president Woodrow Wilson.

By the early 1920s, with the advice and assistance of the Communist International established by the Bolsheviks to aid in the development of revolutionary movements around the world, a small but dedicated group of Chinese Marxist intellectuals and workers established the Communist Party of China (CPC). Over the next three decades, the CPC struggled to build a mass movement to overthrow the old powers within Chinese society and to drive out the foreign imperialists who had been bleeding the country of its wealth for more than a hundred years. After a brief alliance in the United Front of 1923–1927, the Communists were locked into a contest to determine whether China could bring an end to the twin oppressions of the domestic and international orders and find a path to a future of independence and socialist development. Surviving both the repeated "extermination campaigns" of the Nationalists under Chiang Kai-shek (Jiang Jieshi) and the brutal invasion and occupation of much of the country by Japan, the CPC and the Red Army were able to carry through the final efforts of liberation and cross the threshold of a new era with the founding of the People's Republic. They then faced the immense challenges of actually bringing about the building of a New China, and creating a new place for their country in the world. Over the past seventy-five years China's history has been shaped by the dialectic between domestic development and international relations. This is the story to be told in this book.

Three major phases can be discerned in this history, each of which can be further divided into two or three segments. The first phase starts from the founding of the PRC in 1949 to the transition from the leadership of Mao Zedong to that of Deng Xiaoping in 1976–1978, with the periods of 1949–1959, 1959–1966, and 1966–1978 as discrete subdivisions. Across these years, the Chinese leadership struggled to find a path of socialist construction, to position the country in its relationships with both the US-dominated capitalist world and the socialist camp led by the Soviet Union, as well as to find a place amongst the newly emerging nations of the postcolonial world. The second major phase goes from 1979–2011, with the shorter segments of 1979–1989, 1989–1997, and 1997–2011 as its components. During this phase, China settled on the course of reform and opening, and adopted a posture of accommodation with the global capitalist system while working to build its economic and political capabilities. Finally, there is the current era, beginning in 2011 and continuing to the time of this writing in 2024, which can usefully be divided into two periods, from 2011 to 2020, and from 2020 to 2024. This is the era of the leadership of Xi Jinping, when China had achieved sufficient development to no longer need to assume a deferential posture towards the West, and could begin to reclaim a significant role in world affairs. These units will form the chapters to follow.

PART ONE

CHAPTER 1: 1949–1959

The establishment of the new government of the People's Republic of China faced immediate challenges. The country was devastated by years of warfare with millions of people displaced, the economy in the grips of massive inflation, and the menace of possible military intervention by the United States. The first priority for the leadership was to stabilize the economy and bring security to the people. In order to do this, they decided to appeal to the Soviet Union for assistance. In December 1949, Mao Zedong and a delegation of negotiators traveled by train to Moscow with the objective of signing a treaty of friendship and mutual support with the Soviet Union. This was Mao's first trip ever outside China, and one of only two he would make in his life, both to Moscow. In January 1950, Zhou Enlai, who was serving as both prime minister and foreign minister in the new government, joined Mao in Moscow for the later stages of the negotiations.

The relationship between the CPC and the Soviets was complex. Under Stalin's leadership, the Soviets had provided material support to the Nationalist government of Chiang Kai-shek from the 1920s until late in the civil war. The Soviets viewed the Nationalists as the leading political force in China, and consistently urged the CPC to work together with the GMD. In 1945, the Soviet Union had signed a treaty of friendship with Chiang's government in the wake of the defeat of Japan. It was only as it became clear that the Red Army was on the verge of defeating the Nationalist forces in 1948 that Stalin finally cut off aid to Chiang and shifted to strong support for the CPC. At the end of World War II, the Soviet Red Army had occupied

Josef Stalin and Mao Zedong (*center, rear*) at the signing of the Friendship Treaty, 1950. Photo: Alamy Stock Photo

northeast China, which had been the Japanese puppet state of Manchukuo since 1933. Now the Soviets agreed to provide direct assistance to the Chinese revolutionary forces in the area as they prepared for the final confrontation with the Nationalists. But when Mao and Zhou were negotiating with Stalin in Moscow, the memory of earlier Soviet actions would have been strong in their minds.

Stalin was also concerned about the possible effects of a new treaty with China, which would abrogate the 1945 agreement with the Republican government signed as part of the settlement of postwar issues agreed upon by the Allies at Yalta. Under those terms, the Soviet Union was to take control of the Kuril Islands and the southern part of Sakhalin Island from Japan, and Stalin worried that breaking the 1945 treaty would lead the United States to challenge Soviet control in those areas. He also had concerns about the Chinese Eastern Railway and its southern terminus at Lushun, known in the West as Port Arthur, now the city of Dalian, both of which had been under Soviet control since they were seized from Japan at the end of the war.

These negotiations were taking place, of course, in the context of the Cold War. The United States had emerged from World War II as the new dominant power in the capitalist world, supplanting Great Britain as the leading imperialist power in Asia as well. Anticommunism in the United States became the foundation of its foreign policy. US forces in divided Germany were positioned to "contain" further Soviet influence in western Europe and directly confronted the Soviets in Berlin. In East Asia, the Korean peninsula was divided into zones of occupation by the United States and the Soviets, setting the stage for the war soon to follow. In Southeast Asia, the primacy of the Cold War mentality among US policy makers was demonstrated in the difference between the US response to anticolonial struggles in Indonesia and Indochina. In the former, where the anti-Dutch forces were seen by the United States as simple nationalists, the US pushed the Netherlands government to grant independence in 1949. But in Indochina, where the struggle against the French was led by communists, the United States backed the French and, indeed, stepped in to carry on the war when the French had had enough in 1954.

In this context of deepening hostility between the US-led West and the emerging Socialist Bloc with the Soviet Union at its core, the Sino-Soviet negotiations in Moscow in the winter of 1949–1950 took on great significance. Mao and Zhou pressed for a new treaty which would provide economic and technical aid to China as it sought to launch programs of economic development and socialist construction. Stalin eventually overcame his initial concerns, and in February 1950, the two sides reached agreement; on February 14, the new Treaty of Friendship, Alliance, and Mutual Assistance was signed. This laid the foundation for a decade of close cooperation and collaboration between the Soviet Union and China, a period vital to the early stages of socialist development in the People's Republic. The Soviet Union provided loans, machinery and other technical materials, and thousands of advisers and support workers to aid in industrial and military development. For these ten years, the Soviets and the Eastern European socialist states were intimately bound up with China's efforts to build a new economic and social order. As will be seen, this was not an entirely unproblematic set of relationships, and over time disagreements between the Soviet and Chinese leaderships over the course of development in China would lead to a rupture, but for this critical first decade, the Sino-Soviet relationship was truly one of comradely solidarity and a largely shared vision of a socialist future.

While China and the Soviet Union were forging the links which would bind them together through the 1950s, the United States was plunging ever more deeply into the anti-communist hysteria of the McCarthy era. There had been, of course, an alliance between the US and the Soviet Union during World War II, the great anti-fascist struggle. During the war, the United States had also briefly engaged with communist forces in both China and Vietnam who were fighting against Japanese occupiers. The Office of Strategic Services (OSS) sent the Dixie Mission to China and the Deer Mission to Vietnam, and for a while it seemed as though the US might seek a positive relationship with Mao and the CPC in a postwar China, and with Ho Chi Minh in Vietnam. But when President Franklin Roosevelt died in April 1945 and Harry Truman assumed the presidency, US foreign policy shifted dramatically in the anti-communist direction. As the Cold War set in, the United States turned decisively against the revolutions in Asia. When the Communist Party came to power in China, there was a frantic purge of diplomats and others in the State Department who were blamed for the United States' "loss of China." The US also carried out vicious attacks on leftist elements in its occupation zone in southern Korea and installed a puppet government, the Republic of Korea (ROK), led by Syngman Rhee, a conservative Christian preacher who had not lived in the country since 1896.

Korea was to become the first flashpoint in the United States' campaign to "contain" communism in Asia as part of its overall Cold War strategy. While the north became the seat of the popular Democratic People's Republic of Korea (DPRK) with Kim Il Sung as its leader, the US created a repressive police state in the south. In 1948, both the Soviet and US troops which had been stationed in Korea since Japan's surrender in August 1945 were withdrawn. Tensions soon heightened between the two parts of the peninsula, further intensified with the victory of the revolution in China and the rising tide of anti-communist paranoia in the United States, which maintained a large military presence in Japan even after the formal end of the postwar occupation. By early 1950, leaders in the DPRK were deeply concerned that an invasion from the south was a real possibility.

For China, this was an especially troubling situation. Having just brought the long revolutionary struggle to a successful conclusion, and with the hope for a future of development aided by the Soviet Union, China wanted and needed peace. During the negotiations for the Sino-Soviet treaty Mao Zedong had remarked to Stalin:

The most important question at the present time is the question of establishing peace. China needs a period of three to five years of peace, which would be used to bring the economy back to prewar levels, and to stabilize the country in general. Decisions and the most important questions in China hinge on the prospects for a peaceful future. With this in mind, with Central Committee of the Communist Party of China entrusted me to ascertain from you, comrade Stalin, in what way and for how long will international peace be preserved?

Stalin replied to this by noting that at that time there was no immediate threat of war, unless, he joked, Kim Il Sung should invade China.

On Sunday, June 25, 1950, war broke out not with an invasion of China, but with a preemptive strike by North Korea across the line of demarcation with the south, which led to the capture of Seoul by DPRK forces within three days. The United States reacted quickly, mobilizing its allies within the United Nations to vote for sending military forces to support the US-sponsored regime of Syngman Rhee. The north achieved initial successes, pushing ROK forces into a small pocket centered on Busan in the far south. But in mid-September, US forces commanded by General Douglas MacArthur landed at Inchon, well behind the front line of DPRK forces, splitting the northern armies in two and shifting the tide of battle. By late October, DPRK troops had been pushed back almost to the border with China, and MacArthur was calling for extending the war into China to overthrow the new government there.

China's hopes for a long period of peace to enable the country to get on its feet and begin the process of socialist construction had been thoroughly derailed. Once the conflict had begun, there was period of debate and consultation both within the CPC and between the Chinese and the Soviets about how to respond. China was reluctant to be drawn into a new war, which would drain resources desperately needed by its own people. But it was hardly possible to turn away from supporting the DPRK, given both the long historical and cultural links between Korea and China, and the imperatives of socialist solidarity. Once US intervention had reversed the fortunes of the northern armies, it was virtually impossible for China to fail to

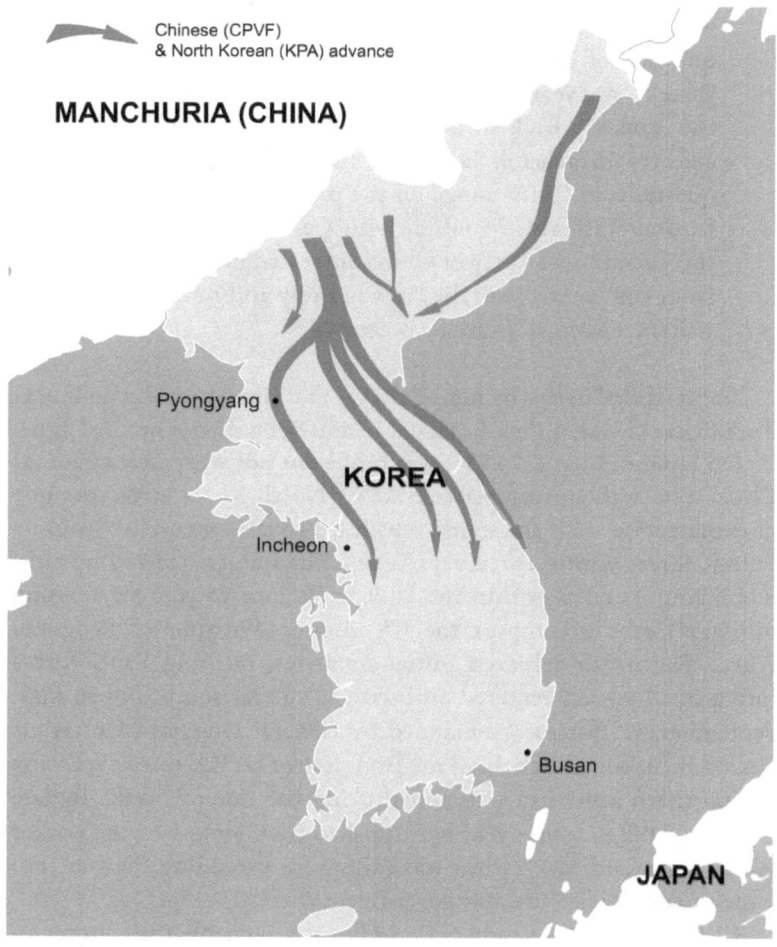

Map showing the advance of Chinese and North Korean forces, 1950. Map: Tina Duong

extend direct military assistance. In late October, some six hundred thousand Chinese People's Volunteers crossed into Korea and began to engage with US forces, which were soon driven back south until the war settled into a prolonged clash around the middle of the peninsula.

Beyond sending its army to fight in Korea, the United States also pursued other anti-China activities. President Truman ordered the US Navy to patrol the waters of the Taiwan Strait in order to prevent any effort by the People's Liberation Army to liberate Taiwan from

Zhou Enlai in Geneva, 1954. Photo: Alamy Stock Photo

the rump regime of the Nationalists. Chiang Kai-shek had withdrawn his forces there from 1948–1949, having first, in February 1948, savagely repressed protests by Taiwanese people opposed to having their island become the haven of the defeated Guomindang. By sending the navy into the strait, Truman began direct US intervention in the final moments of the Chinese Civil War and propped up the Nationalist leftovers, a policy which has been carried forward until the present day. Additionally, the Central Intelligence Agency (CIA) worked with the Guomindang military to carry out raids on the China coast, and flew bombing missions over Shanghai well into the early 1950s. The United States' hostility towards China was comprehensive and persistent throughout the 1950s and '60s.

The war in Korea dragged on for three years. An armistice, bringing an end to the fighting but leaving the underlying political issues of the divided peninsula unaddressed, was signed on June 19, 1953. For China, this was a great relief as it allowed the country to finally focus its energies on economic development and the transition to a socialist system. It also gave Chinese leaders concerned with foreign affairs, led by Zhou Enlai, new chances to develop the country's relations with other postcolonial developing nations. The next two years saw China emerge as a significant participant in international affairs, first at the

Leaders of the Non-Aligned Movement (*From left to right*: PM Pandit Jawaharlal Nehru of India, President Kwame Nkrumah of Ghana, President Gamal Abdel Nasser of Egypt, President Sukarno of Indonesia, and President Josip Broz Tito of Yugoslavia) Photo: Alamy Stock Photo

Geneva Conference of 1954 to address the situations in Korea and Indochina, and then at the first meeting of the Non-Aligned Movement held in Bandung, Indonesia, in 1955. Zhou Enlai also made an important journey to visit several Asian states, including Burma (now Myanmar) and India, late in 1954.

In February 1954, the foreign ministers of the four "great powers," the United States, the Soviet Union, Britain, and France, concluded a meeting in Berlin by calling for the convening of an international conference to attempt to resolve the conflicts in Korea and Indochina. They chose to extend an invitation to China to also take part in these talks. This was a major achievement for the new Chinese government, as it was a de facto recognition that the People's Republic was legitimately one of the important powers concerned. Although the United States' hostility prevented China from taking its rightful place in the United Nations until 1971, the invitation to Geneva was a milestone in socialist China's emergence as significant participant in global affairs.

The Geneva conference opened on April 16. It quickly became apparent that no real progress would be made in addressing the situation in Korea. US intransigence prevented any meaningful discussion.

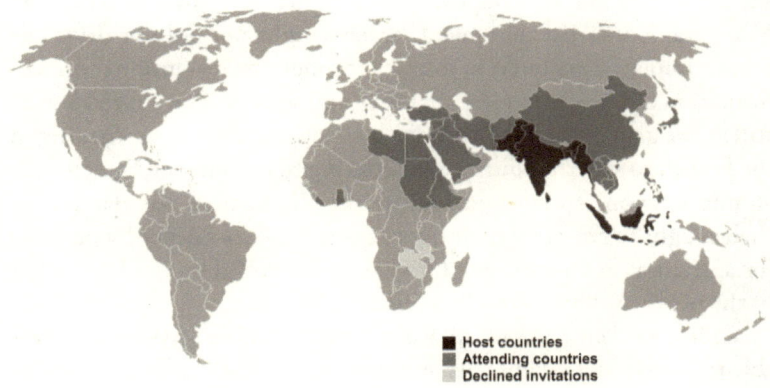

■ Host countries
■ Attending countries
□ Declined invitations

Participants in the 1955 Bandung Conference of the Non-Aligned Movement. Map: Tina Duong

However, the case of Indochina appeared to be much different. In the wake of World War II, the major European colonial powers had found themselves increasingly unable and unwilling to bear the costs of maintaining control of their overseas possessions. As noted above, the Dutch had been driven from Indonesia by the end of 1949. In Indochina, the French, after initially trying to reestablish control following the Japanese surrender in August 1945, had fought a war against the Viet Minh and its allied forces who sought to create independent states in Vietnam, Laos, and Cambodia. But by early 1954, the French government faced both fiscal constraints and rising popular opposition to the war which made them willing to seek an exit strategy.

As the spring of 1954 arrived, Viet Minh forces had pinned down a major French garrison at Dienbienphu, near the border with Laos in northwestern Vietnam. Under the leadership of General Vo Nguyen Giap, the independence fighters besieged the French in a remote valley, doggedly transporting artillery and ammunition over the surrounding rugged mountains and gradually tightening their encirclement of the imperialist position. Finally, on May 7, the French surrendered. News of this capitulation arrived in Geneva on the morning of May 8, just as the conference there turned its attention to the Indochina conflict. The Viet Minh victory changed the tenor of the negotiations, which became a discussion about how the French could extricate themselves and what a postcolonial Indochina would look like. But the United States was opposed to a French withdrawal. The Viet Minh was a socialist movement which sought not only to drive out French imperialism, but also to carry through the revolutionary transformation of the Vietnamese economy and society. The United States, still in the grip of the McCarthyite anti-communist frenzy, first urged the French to stay the course, even offering to provide the French with atomic weapons to be used against the Vietnamese popular forces, then sought to frustrate their hopes for full independence by pushing for a division of the country into zones controlled by the Viet Minh in the north and by a pro-US regime in the south.

China worked hard to obtain the best possible settlement agreeable to all the participants. An eventual agreement was reached under the terms of which Laos and Cambodia would become independent, neutral countries, retaining the traditional monarchical governments. Vietnam would be "temporarily" divided at the seventeenth parallel. In the north, the Viet Minh would establish their new socialist state. In the south, a provisional government would remain in place until nationwide elections could be held in 1956. This was not an ideal resolution, but given the implacable hostility of the US imperialists, it seemed to be the best option. As things turned out, of course, the 1956 elections were never held, as the United States knew Ho Chi Minh and the Viet Minh would easily win and the country would be reunified under a single socialist system. The US set up a puppet government in the south led by Ngo Dinh Diem, a reactionary Catholic who quickly unleashed a campaign of terror against Viet Minh and other anticolonial activists.

In the fall of 1954, however, these developments lay in the future. In the wake of the Geneva conference China set about seeking to resolve two issues relating to its international borders, one with Burma and the other with India, both arising from the legacy of British imperialism in South Asia. India had been taken over piecemeal by the East India Company, a corporation that acted like a state. After the great revolt against foreign rule in 1857, India became a crown colony directly under the control of the British state. Shortly after this Britain extended its imperialist aggression to Burma, which was incorporated into the British Empire in three phases ending in the 1880s. Britain sought to define the borders of these imperial possessions and to maximize the areas under its control. Taking advantage of the weakness of China under the pressure of Western imperialism in the late nineteenth- and early twentieth-century, Britain declared the McMahon line to be the border between their territories and China, though no Chinese government ever actually accepted this delineation.

Through a series of negotiations that took place in New Delhi, Yangon, and Beijing, the Chinese explored various options for resolving the conflicting claims which the postcolonial governments in India and Burma were pursuing. An agreement with Burma was eventually reached in August 1955, but the negotiations with India proved more frustrating. As will be seen, the border issue between China and India would lead to military conflict in 1962, and remains a source of tension between the countries today.

During one set of meetings in New Delhi, Zhou Enlai and the Indian premier Jawaharlal Nehru agreed to issue a joint statement endorsing the Chinese "Five Principles of Peaceful Co-Existence" as the basis for both their state-to-state relations and as a general foundation for relations between countries in general. The Five Principles are: mutual respect for sovereignty and territorial integrity, mutual nonaggression, noninterference in each other's internal affairs, equality and mutual benefit, and peaceful coexistence. These have remained the foundation of China's international relations up to the present time. They were to play a critical role in China's efforts to develop a role for itself as one of the newly independent countries preparing to gather in Bandung, Indonesia, for the first Non-Aligned Movement meeting in 1955.

As countries began to emerge from their colonial bondage, new leaders were seeking paths to development and modernization. China had declared in 1950 that it would "lean to one side" in terms of the division between the socialist world and the US-dominated capitalist West, which of course included the main former colonial powers. But China also saw itself as a postcolonial country, having overthrown the domination not of a single colonial master but of the combined, often-contested oppression of all the Western powers, plus Japan. So as plans for a gathering of newly independent states, seeking to find ways to avoid becoming newly subordinated to either the United States or the Soviets, began to take shape, China wanted to be a part of this movement. India, Egypt, and Indonesia were the main sponsors of the new grouping, but many other former colonies also sought to send delegations. Some of the countries taking part in the planned gathering were wary of China, which was clearly aligned with the Soviet Union through the treaty of friendship and was on an avowedly socialist path of development. In preparing to join the meeting, Zhou Enlai emphasized the Five Principles and highlighted China's position as a poor country with a large population which faced many of the same challenges as other new nations.

The Bandung Conference opened in mid-April 1955. On his way there, Zhou escaped an assassination attempt by US-backed agents of the Taiwan regime who had planted a bomb on the plane he had been scheduled to take from Hong Kong to Jakarta. Later at the conference, he gave a major address to the assembly on April 19, where he once again spoke of the common ground shared by the people of the gathered states and urged the Five Principles as the best basis for building future relations among them. Just as the Geneva negotiations which brought the era of French imperialist rule in Indochina to an end marked China's emergence as a serious participant in global diplomatic affairs, China's engagement with other newly independent countries at Bandung demonstrated the legitimacy and acceptance of the People's Republic by what would come to be called the Third World. In the months following the Bandung conference, China established diplomatic relations with many new countries, including Afghanistan, Cambodia, Ceylon (Sri Lanka), Egypt, Guinea, Iraq, Morocco, Syria, Sudan, and Yemen.

By the mid-1950s, then, China had survived the Korean War, made significant progress in agricultural reform and the development of cooperatives, and, with Soviet aid and assistance, begun the process of building a modern industrial economy. Geneva and Bandung marked the PRC's emergence on the world stage. But new challenges were about to arise. In March 1953, the Soviet leader Stalin died. Over the next couple of years, a new leadership was consolidated with Nikita Khruschev at its core. In February 1956, the Soviet Communist Party convened its Twentieth Congress, at which, on February 25, Khruschev gave what has been called his "secret speech," though it did not remain secret for long. In this four-hour long address, Khruschev denounced Stalin and repudiated many of his actions. This was a dramatic and shocking event for communists, not only in the Soviet

Union, but around the world. For the Chinese leadership it was a particularly thorny problem with which to grapple. As discussed above, the relationship between the CPC and the Soviets under Stalin's leadership had not always been a close one, and even with the signing of the 1950 treaty, the legacy of those tensions lingered. Yet Khruschev's was initially received without serious criticism. Indeed, even into early 1957, the CPC commented in a pamphlet,

> Since the Twentieth Congress of the Communist Party of the Soviet Union, the Soviet people under the correct leadership of the central committee of the Communist Party, headed by Comrade Khruschev, have achieved a series of great successes in building communism.

But the Chinese also observed,

> Stalin displayed a certain great nation chauvinist tendency in relation to brother parties and countries. The essence of such tendencies lies in being unmindful of the independent and equal status of the communist parties of various lands and those of socialist countries.

To begin with, then, the Chinese responded cautiously but with some moderate expressions of concern about the nature of the relationship between the Soviets and themselves. In the wake of Khruschev's speech, developments elsewhere were more dramatic. In Eastern Europe, the immediate effect was for the imperialists to encourage certain anti-communist elements within the socialist states. This led to the uprising in Hungary in October 1956, which was suppressed with the intervention of the Soviet Red Army. China supported the Soviet moves to restore order and preserve the socialist state in Hungary, while internally reflecting on how they saw the situation in Eastern Europe as shaped by the kind of "great nation chauvinism" they had noted in their earlier comments on Stalin.

The Chinese increasingly saw the Soviets under Khruschev as turning away from the path of revolution and embracing the idea of peaceful coexistence with US-led imperialism as the basis of their foreign policies. At the same time, Mao and others were develop-

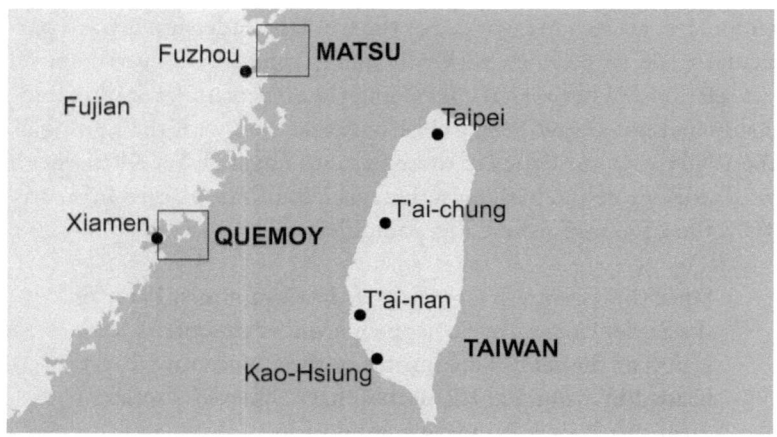

Site of the Taiwan Strait 'crisis,' 1954. Map: Tina Duong

ing a critique of Soviet political economy, which they saw as overly bureaucratic and seriously alienated from the masses. These concerns, and other sources of tension between the Chinese and the Soviets, would intensify towards the end of the 1950s, and lead to the rupture between the two, which deepened through the 1960s.

While these tensions with the Soviets simmered beneath the surface, the United States' hostility towards China continued in full view through the 1950s. After the the Korean war ended, the US focused on securing Japan, South Korea, and Taiwan as its front line for the containment of China. Tens of thousands of US troops were stationed in these areas, the US Navy continued to sail through the Taiwan Strait, and a secret military training camp was set up in Colorado to prepare Tibetan terrorists to be infiltrated from India to foment separatist agitation on the Tibetan Plateau. In 1954, there was a "crisis" when the Nationalist regime on Taiwan deployed seventy-three thousand troops to the islands of Jinmen and Mazu (a.k.a. Quemoy and Matsu), just miles off the coast of Fujian province. In response to this provocation, the People's Liberation Army (PLA) began shelling these islands. At the end of 1954 and the beginning of 1955, China took control of two sets of islands off the coast of Zhejiang which had been held by the Nationalists. The US reacted with predictably aggressive moves, with President Eisenhower even threatening to use nuclear weapons to strike at PLA positions in Fujian.

This confrontation abated in the spring of 1955 as China prepared to take part in the Bandung conference, but in 1958 another, more serious situation arose in the Taiwan Strait.

After the 1954–1955 crisis had subsided, Zhou Enlai had made conciliatory public statements about the desirability of peacefully resolving the Taiwan question, and also pursued several back-channel efforts to communicate with the Nationalist authorities on the island, providing openings for negotiating the peaceful reunification of the country. Mao Zedong even stated that Taiwan would be able to keep its own distinctive set of local political arrangements after reunification, including continuing to use Sun Yat-sen's "Three Principles of the People" as their guiding ideology. But the GMD leaders, backed by the US imperialists, refused to respond to or even acknowledge these overtures. In the summer of 1958, the PLA once again began to shell the nearby offshore islands of Jinmen and Mazu. This continued every day for six weeks, effectively isolating these Nationalist outposts from the main island across the Strait.

One byproduct of the 1954 Geneva talks had been the opening of a discrete line of communication between China and the United States. Private, unannounced meetings were held between the US ambassador to Czechoslovakia and the Chinese ambassador to Poland, which continued until late 1957. As the new confrontation in the Taiwan Strait developed, these talks were renewed, with the US ambassador to Poland now representing the US. There were a number of false starts and miscommunications, but by September, the United States began to weaken its position, and in the end, China suspended the bombardments as part of a "noose strategy," the idea being that by leaving the offshore islands in Nationalist hands, even though they could easily have been liberated by the PLA, the GMD authorities and their US backers would remain tied to these close links to the mainland. Chiang Kai-shek and the United States hoped to trade the abandonment of Jinmen and Mazu for an agreement by the PRC to renounce the possible use of force to liberate Taiwan. This was unacceptable, so Mao and Zhou devised the "noose strategy" to keep their options open.

By 1959, New China was completing its first decade. Much had been accomplished, despite serious challenges and deepening disagreements among the leadership of the CPC about the best path of socialist development to follow. The lives of the more than six hundred million Chinese people had been steadily improved. Life expectancy had risen, infant mortality had declined, housing, education, and basic health care had been greatly advanced. In the agricultural economy, a steady, incremental process of collectivization had yielded regular rises in grain production. And the industrial sector had been given a strong foundation, especially in core heavy industry, with significant assistance from the Soviet Union. But 1959 proved to be a year of many challenges, both domestically and internationally.

Beginning in 1958, a wave of enthusiasm for further agricultural collectivization swept across China. New large units called People's Communes began to be formed, a process which accelerated rapidly after Mao Zedong commented during an inspection tour, "People's Communes are good!" This became the beginning of the Great Leap Forward, an effort to mobilize the creative energies of the people to achieve breakthroughs in economic development, which took off in the winter of 1958–1959. While in many ways this built on the successes of the previous years, contradictions soon emerged which led to a major crisis. This was a combination of bureaucratic distortion in the reporting of grain output, as lower and middle level cadres sought to bolster their performance by slightly exaggerating production figures, which in the course of reporting up the administrative hierarchy became seriously distorted accounts, leading to excessive procurement for urban consumption and sale in the international grain markets. This in turn left inadequate supplies in the hands of the communes. To make matters worse, the weather, which had been steadily mild for most of the 1950s, turned bad and harvests suffered. By early 1959, food shortages began to cause serious malnutrition, and in some areas, starvation. Ultimately millions of people died, though nothing like the many tens of millions touted by hostile elements in the West.

The CPC faced serious problems in responding to the contradictions arising from the Great Leap. Disagreements among party leaders about the best path of socialist development had been deepening through the 1950s, with Mao and his associates emphasizing mass mobilization, while Liu Shaoqi, Deng Xiaoping, and others saw development as a complex and challenging process which required the deployment of special skills and talents. All agreed on the goal of building a modern socialist economy, but how to do this was a matter of increasing contention. At a plenary meeting of the leadership at

Lushan in the summer of 1959, these tensions led to a serious political confrontation, as a result of which Peng Dehuai, who had been
Minister of Defense and was a critic of the Maoist model, had to step
down, but Mao also had to withdraw from day-to-day leadership of
state and party affairs. This set the stage for further conflict among
the leadership, which would culminate with the Cultural Revolution
and its aftermath, as will be discussed below.

While these internal contradictions were unfolding, China's
relationship with the Soviet Union was also undergoing significant
change. While the Soviets had provided large-scale financial, material,
and technical aid to China throughout the '50s which were vital to
China's efforts to launch its process of socialist development, many
in the Soviet leadership, especially once Khruschev emerged as the
key figure, were uncomfortable with the direction China was taking,
and especially with the mass mobilization approach favored by Mao
and his associates. And as we have noted above, Mao and others in
China were increasingly anxious about what they perceived to be the
excessive bureaucratization of the Soviet Communist Party and the
government of the Soviet Union, which they saw as alienated from
the masses and in effect forming a new elite. These anxieties would
contribute directly to the launching of the Cultural Revolution.

As the Great Leap Forward got underway, Soviet criticism of
China's development strategy reached a breaking point. Minor ten-
sions over issues like loan repayment schedules and other technical
issues had emerged as early as 1957, but in the summer of 1959, as the
CPC was grappling with the contradictions developing around the
Great Leap, the Soviets announced that they were suspending their
program of assisting China in developing their own atomic bomb.
A year later, while China was still recovering from the effects of the
Great Leap, in July 1960 the Soviets terminated their aid programs
and withdrew some thirteen thousand advisors from China. This
deeply affected China's overall development programs and was especially harmful in the context of the Great Leap Forward, perhaps
intended to undermine Mao's position as preeminent leader. These
measures effectively mark the beginning of the Sino-Soviet split,
which would deepen through the next decade.

One final set of events added to the turmoil of 1959. In March,
monastic elements in Lhasa staged a rebellion, despite the fact that

the central government in Beijing had given the Tibet Autonomous Region comprehensive exemption from major policies such as land reform and socialist modernization, allowing the theocratic local administration headed by the Dalai Lama to continue as the effective administrators of local affairs. Tibet had been part of the old imperial system of China, particularly since the late seventeenth century, when the Qing dynasty sent military forces to Lhasa to support the local authorities against invasions from Nepal. Throughout the Qing era the relationship between the religious elites in Tibet and the Manchu rulers in Beijing had been close, and as Western imperialists established their dominance over China in the nineteenth century Tibet was clearly recognized as part of the Qing empire. When the Qing dynasty collapsed in 1911–1912 the faltering central governments which succeeded it did not exercise extensive control in Tibet, and the local theocrats maintained a functional autonomy between 1912 and 1949. But once the People's Republic was established, and as the PLA brought the far-flung regions of China under central authority, the position of Tibet became a focus of concern for the new government. The CPC and state leaders were anxious to ensure the security and stability of China's borders, and to establish the sovereignty and territorial integrity of the country. In 1950, units of the PLA moved up to the Tibetan Plateau to secure the border with India and ensure stability in the region.

The central government entered into discussion with the local authorities in Tibet about how to manage the relationship between the region and the rest of the country. Tibet was a theocratic society— that is to say there had been no "separation of church and state" and that the religious authority of the monasteries was the supreme power in the land. Political leadership was shared between two supreme spiritual figures, the Dalai Lama and the Panchen Lama, with the Dalai Lama as the more prominent of the two. At this time, the Dalai Lama was a young man, just sixteen years old. Guided by a council of advisors, he served as the top authority in the discussions between the central and local authorities. Agreements were reached which established the stability of the country and secured the territorial integrity of China's borders, while allowing the local religious powers to continue to serve as the administrators of the region and exempting Tibet from central policies for the foreseeable future.

These agreements were honored throughout the 1950s. In areas of Sichuan province, adjacent to Tibet where a number of Tibetans resided, central government programs of land reform and agricultural collectivization did apply, and the power of local monastic institutions was curtailed. This led to tensions and occasional clashes between some Tibetan elements and the local and provincial governments. At the same time, as noted above, the United States, as part of its overall posture of hostility to China, was running a training program for Tibetan separatist terrorist groups in Colorado and infiltrating them into Tibet through India to carry out sabotage and agitation against the central government. This was the background for the revolt of March 1959.

The basis for the revolt was the fear on the part of monastic authorities that they would lose the power they had historically exercised over Tibetan society and the economic privileges which they had enjoyed as leaders of the religious institutions which concentrated the wealth produced by working people in the hands of the Buddhist elites. The Dalai Lama, by now a grown man in his mid-twenties, fled to India, his escape allowed by the PLA, which did not pursue him as he traveled over the Himalaya mountains. The uprising was quickly brought under control, but the establishment of a "government in exile" by the Dalai Lama in Dharmsala, India, became a point of friction between China and India and of leverage for the United States in its ongoing demonization campaigns directed at China. The US terrorist training program in Colorado continued until the 1970s, and Tibet has remained an important rhetorical trope to be invoked by anti-China forces in the West.

The 1950s saw China regain its independence and begin to develop its economy, improving the livelihoods of its people, and beginning to take its place on the stage of world affairs. The alliance with the Soviet Union provided critical inputs to get China's development going. The war in Korea put great stress on People's China in the very first years of its existence, but the country made great sacrifices to assist its neighbors in the DPRK in resisting US imperialism. China was able to step forward into a global role at the Geneva Conference in 1954 and the first meeting of the Non-Aligned Movement at Bandung in 1955, establishing the Five Principles of Peaceful Coexistence as the basis for its international relations. The two relationships with the Soviet Union and the United States were most critical for China during these years, but there were also important interactions with India, countries in Southeast Asia, and Africa. By the end of the decade stresses had built up with the Soviets which led to the split of 1959–1960 and which would deepen in the 1960s. The first half of that decade will be the subject of the next chapter.

CHAPTER 2: 1960–1965

The first half of the 1960s was a period of turmoil in China's domestic political affairs and of rapid transformations in the international environment. The tensions over the best path forward in socialist construction continued to deepen among leaders of the Communist Party, with Mao Zedong somewhat marginalized from the daily management of affairs, but still feeling profound concerns about bureaucratization and the alienation of the party from the masses. The Socialist Education Movement of 1962–1963 was an effort to shake up the cadres in rural work, but Mao felt frustrated with its outcome and worried about the long-term future of the country. Meanwhile, the economy recovered from the disruptions of the Great Leap Forward and the advocates of a more deliberate pace of development worked towards further technological and industrial advances in the wake of the withdrawal of Soviet support. The relationship with the Soviet Union continued to deteriorate in the early years of the decade. At the same time, the United States maintained its hostile posture towards China, and by the middle of the '60s had launched its full-scale imperialist war in Vietnam. China also faced serious crises in its relationships with India and Indonesia, while in a more positive vein it began to develop ongoing engagements in Africa.

The sudden cutting off of aid from the Soviets and the almost overnight departure of thousands of Soviet advisors in 1960 was a great shock, both to the Chinese and to many of the Soviet citizens who had come to the country and had developed close relationships of solidarity with their local counterparts. One such advisor, a prominent Soviet scientist named Mikhail Klochko, later wrote about the surprise and disorientation he had felt, which was shared by many of his comrades and colleagues:

> As one of those who was suddenly and surprisingly ordered home in 1960, I can testify that all of the anger at the move was not limited to the Chinese. Without exception, my fellow scientists and the other Soviet specialists whom I knew in China were extremely upset at being recalled before the end of our contracts. Like myself, others must have had difficulty hiding their amazement when told by Soviet representatives in Beijing that dissatisfaction with our living and working conditions was an important reason for our recall. In fact, a few of us had never lived better in our whole lives than we did in China. Our Chinese hosts were even more mystified. Again and again they asked [us] why we are we leaving and whether anything could be done to prevent our going. The suddenness with which the events developed indicated that the decision was irreversible.

The blow to China was of course not just a matter of these disrupted relationships, but had an immediate and very practical impact on investment and construction projects across the country, among them China's efforts to develop its own nuclear weapons program.

Over the next two years, the Communist Party of China and Soviet Party exchanged a series of polemical letters setting out their mutual concerns and criticisms. Sometime the ideological messages were somewhat indirect, as with a pair of pamphlets published by the Chinese in December 1961 and March 1963 which formally addressed "The Differences Between Comrade Togliatti and Us," presenting Chinese criticisms as directed towards the leader of the Italian Communist Party rather than the Soviets. But in other instances, the exchanges were direct between the Central Committees of the two parties. During this period, the conflicts between the Soviets and the Chinese continued to be articulated as disagreements between comrades, but as the decade advanced, it morphed more and more into an antagonism between national states. This is important to note, as it reflects the reality that China's relations with other countries, as was also true for the Soviet Union, were shaped both by the socialist ideology which animated their respective revolutionary histories, and by considerations distinct from their Marxist principles, more rooted in geography and culture than in theoretical propositions.

China's concerns with the Soviets encompassed two main themes. One was the divergence of approaches to socialist development, which has been discussed already. The other was a deepening anxiety about the position of the Soviet leadership towards their relations with the United States and their commitment to world revolution. Beginning with Khruschev's speech at the Twentieth Party Congress in 1956, the Soviet Union had placed increasing emphasis on the idea of "peaceful coexistence" with US imperialism. As presented by the Soviets, the idea was that in the age of atomic weapons there was a real potential for a war in which nuclear exchanges would take place that could lead to the destruction of most, if not all, human life on earth. This meant that it was necessary to avoid war and seek peace above all else. The superiority of the socialist system would be demonstrated not through military confrontation, but through the slow and steady success of the growing Soviet economy in raising the material standard of living of the Soviet people, an idea which was strongly proposed by Khruschev in 1959 in the "kitchen debate" which took place at an industrial exhibition during US vice president Richard Nixon's visit to Moscow.

The Chinese saw the Soviets' turn to peaceful coexistence as an abandonment of revolutionary struggle and an unacceptable compromise with US imperialism. They saw the Soviets as lowering the level of contradiction between themselves and the United States, while the US continued to pursue its aggressive campaigns of isolation and invasion directed at China and other Asian peoples. In 1960, Khruschev and US president Dwight Eisenhower agreed to a summit meeting to be held in Paris, the first such direct talks between Soviet and US leaders since the end of World War II. This only added to Chinese fears of further reconciliation between the Soviets and the US. In the end the summit did not take place because a US U-2 spy plane was shot down over the Soviet Union, and Khruschev cancelled the talks in retaliation. Nonetheless, relations between the Soviet Union and the United States continued to move in a more conciliatory direction.

Chinese nuclear test at Lop Nur, 1964. Photo: Wikimedia Commons, 人民画报

The Cuban Missile Crisis of October 1962, which brought the world to the brink of nuclear catastrophe, was resolved when Khruschev decided to withdraw Soviet missiles from Cuba in exchange for the US doing the same with missiles it had placed along the Soviet border in Turkey. This was followed in the next year by the signing of the Nuclear Test Ban Treaty, an effort on the part of the countries which already possessed atomic weapons to prevent others from developing them. China, however, was not a party to this agreement. Nor was China invited to take part in further nuclear negotiations later in the '60s, which yielded the Non-Proliferation Treaty, an even more explicit effort by the established atomic powers to close the door to further acquisition of nuclear capabilities by other countries.

As China's anxieties about both US imperialism and the declining relationship with the Soviets deepened, the desire to have a credible nuclear deterrent of their own drove a major effort of research, leading to the testing of their first atomic bomb in October 1964. This was a significant demonstration of both China's determination to pursue its own course and of its increasing capabilities in doing so. As fate would have it, at almost exactly the same time China was attaining this technological breakthrough, Khruschev was being removed from his leading position in the Soviet Union. While this was not the result of any actions or interventions by the Chinese, it was seen, at least initially, as a positive development. But it soon became clear that the new Soviet leadership was actually committed to further reducing tensions with the US. By the middle of the decade, Chinese worries about the Soviet Union were growing steadily more serious.

During these years, the United States maintained its antagonistic attitude towards China and grew increasingly engaged in military actions in Southeast Asia. When France gave up its efforts to restore colonial rule in Indochina after World War II, the US stepped into the imperialist vacuum, initially through propping up the Diem regime in the south, then by canceling the scheduled 1956 elections, and then, with the assumption of the presidency by John Kennedy in 1961, by sending small but increasing numbers of military "advisors" to train and fight alongside the Diem armed forces. US leaders talked about their "domino theory" that if one country in Southeast Asia were to "go communist" then others would follow, and US domination in the region would be undermined. In the 1950s, the US orchestrated the creation of the Southeast Asia Treaty Organization (SEATO) as a local anti-communist imitation of the anti-Soviet North Atlantic Treaty Organization (NATO) in Europe. These efforts to "contain the spread of communism" were all in fact projections of US imperialist power, seeking to dominate and control countries in every part of the world.

Despite US support for the Diem regime, the struggle for independence in southern Vietnam continued, as did efforts by the Pathet Lao, the communist movement in Laos, to overthrow the royal government and create a new socialist state. As these popular movements grew, the US leaders became increasingly concerned that the situation, especially in southern Vietnam, would get out of their control. On November 1, 1963, a military coup, backed by the CIA, overthrew Diem, who had come to be seen as an obstacle to US interests. Instead, they replaced him with the first of a series of petty military figures, none of whom had the slightest chance of establishing any kind of a legitimate popular government. The military forces of the southern regime were not effective in the field, and the independence fighters of the National Liberation Front were making steady gains in controlling much of the countryside. By 1964, US political and military leaders, fearing the "loss of Vietnam," became convinced that only direct US military intervention could forestall a communist victory.

In August 1964, as President Lyndon Johnson was facing reelection, the US Navy, which had been operating in North Vietnamese waters in support of clandestine terrorist operations in the north, staged a couple of "incidents" in the Gulf of Tonkin, as North Vietnamese coast guard vessels sought to challenge their illegal activities. This gave Johnson the pretext to have Congress pass the Gulf of Tonkin Resolution, which bypassed the US Constitution and gave the president unregulated war powers. Johnson immediately began preparing for massive escalation of the United States' war effort, and by the spring of 1965, hundreds of thousands of US troops were being deployed to Vietnam to prop up the southern puppet government in an effort to maintain imperialist control in at least part of the country. While the conflict was taking place in Vietnam, Johnson and other US politicians made it clear in their pronouncements that the real objective of US power was the containment of China.

While US hostility towards China intensified and relations with the Soviet Union grew increasingly strained, developments on the border with India gave rise to a new crisis in 1962. As discussed in chapter one, after liberation, China sought to secure its borders in order to guarantee its own territorial integrity. When Western imperialism swept into Asia in the nineteenth century, one of its impacts was an obsession with delineating borders and maximizing the areas under the control of each of the colonial powers. In the postcolonial era, this left a legacy of conflicting claims, with China facing several along its extensive international frontiers. Some of these were resolved fairly quickly through negotiations, as was the case with Burma noted above. In other instances, these became points of contention. This was the case on the long border between China and the Soviet Union, which would lead to serious conflict at the end of the 1960s, discussed in the next chapter.

China's relations with the newly independent government of India were initially quite close. India had been subjected to British rule, first under the East India Company and then, after 1857, as a crown colony with Queen Victoria assuming the title "Empress of India." Even before this, the British had sought to push their control further and further into Inner Asia, attempting invasions of Afghanistan, and bringing Burma under its domination. British ambitions also extended over the Himalaya Mountains to Tibet, which they hoped to detach from the Qing dynasty. During the late nineteenth and early twentieth centuries, Britain was engaged in what is sometimes called the "Great Game," an imperialist competition with the Russian Czarist empire that was also expanding in Central Asia and in the Western Pacific. Both countries established spying operations in Kashgar in far western China, and Tibet became a focus of their aspirations. In 1904, the British sent a military expedition into Tibet, led by Francis Younghusband. Lhasa was occupied and many Tibetans were killed resisting the foreign invasion.

In India, anticolonial political agitation had begun with the formation of the Indian National Congress in the 1880s. Frustration with British rule and anger over the brutality of the colonial state fueled the growth of the movement through the early twentieth century. In the wake of the two world wars, Britain found itself unable, and under the Labour government unwilling, to bear the costs, both financial and moral, of colonial oppression. The exit from India was precipitous and left the wreckage of the Partition of India in its wake: the area which had been British India was divided into the successor states of India and Pakistan, which involved major, often horrifically violent, population transfers. The new Indian government consolidated its rule at the end of the 1940s just as the revolution in China was reaching its conclusion with the founding of the PRC in 1949.

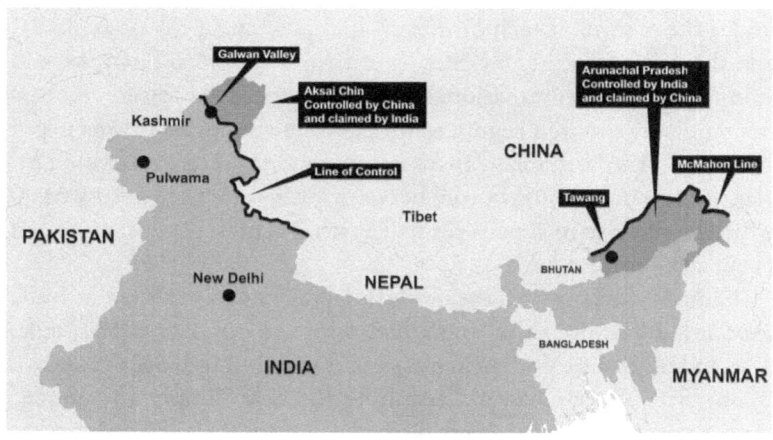

Contested border areas of China and India, 1962. Map: Tina Duong

These two countries, both having thrown off the yoke of imperialism, naturally saw in each other kindred spirits.

Beginning in 1954, Zhou Enlai visited India several times for talks with Prime Minister Nehru. India supported China's participation in the Non-Aligned meetings at Bandung in 1955. Zhou returned to New Delhi several times later in the '50s. But while China had settled its border issues with Burma, which had also been part of the British empire in south Asia, Nehru was unwilling to reach a similar resolution. As the '50s came to a close, Nehru's attitude towards China hardened, and what had been a friendly association with Zhou Enlai deteriorated. India had taken over some of the old British ambitions and was reluctant to give up territorial claims which were solely based on the former imperialist's positions. China hoped to settle the border on the basis of the "line of actual control," meaning the positions actually occupied by each side. This was important in different ways in the two main sectors of the border, in the east beyond Bhutan and in the west north of Kashmir. In the east, China's actual control fell short of the line claimed by the People's Republic, while in the west, China's control of the Aksai Chin region was disputed by India. In the first years of the 1960s, tensions in both areas escalated.

In the summer of 1962, India began moving troops closer to the contested border, and in some instances, began to occupy territory in the west which was not only claimed by China but which had been in the actual control of the country. In several places, Chinese forces withdrew rather than risk violent confrontations with Indian troops. But after a few weeks, the PLA decided enough was enough. On July 21, Chinese troops fired warning shots over Indian soldiers who were advancing towards their positions. This led to a brief cessation of Indian activities and flurry of diplomatic activity. But the underlying differences in the Indian and Chinese positions remained unresolved. Indian efforts to push into Chinese-controlled territories resumed, and Nehru became increasingly provocative in his public statements, saying that his instructions to the army were to "free our territory." The Chinese read this as a clear declaration of India's intentions to launch a campaign of aggression. They decided to preempt this possibility.

The Chinese launched an offensive strike into Indian-claimed areas on October 20. In just three days, all the areas which had been occupied by India had been retaken. In the eastern sector, China gained control of all the areas it claimed down to the McMahon Line and beyond. While India's military was decisively defeated in these contacts, China did not seek to pursue a military solution. Though Nehru continued to issue blustery statements, largely for domestic political consumption, China announced that the PLA would unilaterally cease fighting on November 22, and that on December 1, they would begin to withdraw their forces to the line of actual control as it existed on November 7, 1959. China's commitment to the Five Principles of Peaceful Coexistence, based on respect for the sovereignty and territorial integrity of all countries, was clearly demonstrated in these actions. Sadly, the border issues between India and China remain unresolved down to the present day.

Through the early 1960s, the expanding war in Vietnam was the most visible arena in which the US sought to confront China, but other efforts by the United States also continued. Massive military and economic support for the rump GMD rulers on Taiwan was carried on and steadily increased. Clandestine terrorist operations were run in various parts of China, including the coast across from Taiwan, and in Tibet and Xinjiang. The US also maintained regular U-2 spy plane flights over the country, gathering information and developing targeting models for US nuclear weapons. All of this, of course, contributed to China's concerns about possible direct aggression by the US at the same time as they were, as discussed above, feeling ever-greater anxiety about the role of the Soviet Union. And yet this was not the full extent of US actions directed against China and communist movements elsewhere in Asia. In the vast archipelago of Indonesia, the CIA was, in the first half of the 1960s, increasingly worried about the political influence of the Indonesian Communist Party (PKI) and actively engaged in pursuing efforts to destroy it.

Indonesia was a new country. Like many former colonial possessions of European states, Indonesia emerged from imperialist rule as a single entity where, before the Dutch imposed their power in the nineteenth century, there had been many local political societies. The island of Java alone had several separate sultanates: Bali was a Hindu kingdom and many of the outer islands had little in the way of formal governmental infrastructure. The Dutch created institutions of colonial administration and treated the vast archipelago as a single unit, with little regard for local cultures, languages, or spiritual beliefs. As the anticolonial movement developed at the end of the nineteenth and beginning of the twentieth centuries, a colony-wide nationalism took shape, led by figures like Sukarno and Mohammed Hata. During World War II, the Dutch East Indies were occupied by Japan, and at first the nationalists collaborated with the Japanese in a shared opposition to Western imperialism. As it became clear Japan would lose the war, the Indonesian leaders realized they would have to fight the Dutch in the postwar era, and split with the Japanese in order to better prepare for the war to come. In that struggle, the Dutch steadily lost ground and also faced political pressure from the US to abandon their efforts to reimpose colonial rule. The United States generally opposed European colonialism because it excluded or marginalized US corporate interests from markets and resources in the areas under colonial control. The United States sought a world where capital could flow freely where it had the greatest options for growth and accumulation. Acceding to US wishes, the Dutch granted Indonesia independence at the end of 1949, in sharp contrast to the anti-communist driven support for the French in Indochina, discussed above.

After independence, Indonesia sought to chart its own course of future development. It hosted and was a leading force in the first meeting of the Non-Aligned Movement at Bandung in 1955. Sukarno, who became president of the country, initially pursued a middle course in his economic policies, but he faced demands from the United States to open markets to their investors. Indonesia also was home to the largest communist party, the PKI, outside the socialist bloc. The PKI became increasingly influential in national politics, and Sukarno began to lean more and more towards China in international relations. A series of meetings and diplomatic engagements in the late 1950s and early '60s led to a political alliance of Sukarno and the PKI in 1963. Sukarno was well-aware of US actions in Vietnam and elsewhere in Asia, and wanted to avoid US domination. As he was attempting to do this, the CIA was hard at work preparing to facilitate exactly the fate Sukarno sought to escape.

On September 30, 1965, the Indonesian military launched a coup d'état, arguing that they were moving to preempt a communist takeover of the government. Over the following weeks, the army, assisted by large anti-communist paramilitary groups, carried out not just a coup, but a massive massacre of members of the PKI, leftist workers and intellectuals, people of Chinese ancestry (who were simply assumed to be communists), and others. Around one million people were brutally murdered, and many tens of thousands of other were injured, jailed, or simply disappeared. The initial lists of people to be targeted had been generated in part by CIA operatives working with the Indonesian military. In the wake of the bloodbath, one of the generals, Suharto, became the new "president" and would wield power in the country until he was deposed by a popular movement in 1998.

The destruction of the PKI and the imposition of a military dictatorship radically changed the politics, not only of Indonesia, but of the wider region. Occurring as the US was massively escalating its imperialist war in Vietnam and expanding its military presence from Japan and Korea to the Philippines and Thailand, the events of late 1965 were a serious blow to China. The sense of encirclement by the imperialists became much more palpable. The first years of the 1960s had proven to be ones of challenges and increasing anxiety for Chinese leaders. There was, however, one area in which China was having much more positive experiences, building new relationship and making real contributions to the emergence of postcolonial states and their ability to embark on their own paths of development. This was Africa.

Africa was the last arena in which the European colonial powers sought to carve out territories to be exploited. The "scramble for Africa" in the later years of the nineteenth century culminated with the Congress of Berlin in 1884–1885, where a gathering of imperialists parceled out the lands of African people among themselves, leaving only Ethiopia and Liberia outside the direct rule of one or another Western empire. For the next eighty years or so, Africa was systematically looted and deliberately underdeveloped as a source of raw materials for European industries and as captive markets for the products of factories from Manchester to Dresden. As in the Dutch East Indies, the Europeans created political units to suit their own administrative and economic agendas, creating countries like Kenya or Cameroon where there had previously been complex and diverse local societies. These became the postcolonial states of the 1950s and 1960s, when African peoples were attaining independence either through rebellion, as in Kenya and Algeria, or by political agitation and negotiation, as in Ghana or Senegal.

While some parts of Africa retained links to their former colonial rulers, radical movements for social change and economic development arose in other areas. Socialist and communist movements grew, and China was eager to be of assistance in places where the new governments were seeking aid without having to become subordinate to US power. Many African countries joined the Non-Aligned Movement which China strongly supported. As more and more peoples across the continent became independent, China began to develop links with several of them, which would lead to major projects of infrastructure development and other forms of assistance. These efforts escalated in December 1963 when Zhou Enlai undertook an extended diplomatic tour of Africa, including Egypt, Algeria, Tunisia, and Morocco in North Africa. He went on to visit Ghana, where the president, Kwame Nkrumah, was a close friend of China. He also made stops in Mali and Guinea, which had been the first sub-Saharan country to establish diplomatic relations with the People's Republic. Guinea's leader, Sékou Touré, had been an important voice in Africa speaking out in support of China during the border war with India as well. Zhou went to conclude this tour with visits to Sudan, Ethiopia, and Somalia. In the course of these visits, Zhou spoke regularly about the Five Principles of Peaceful Coexistence, emphasizing the need to respect the sovereignty and territorial integrity of all countries. These visits were also the occasion for the signing of numerous agreements for economic aid and development projects, the beginning of a long, continuing commitment on China's part to the peoples of Africa.

Perhaps the greatest instance of China's aid to Africa in this first phase was the building of a railway in Tanzania and Zambia, often called the Tanzam Railway. In February 1965, Julius Nyerere, the president of Tanzania, which had just become independent from Britain in 1961, made a visit to Beijing. In meetings with Liu Shaoqi and others, the idea of such a railway was first proposed: it would link the port of Dar es Salaam, the capital of Tanzania, with the landlocked interior of Zambia, creating vital infrastructure for the mutual development of both countries. The actual construction of the railway did not take place until 1970–1975, but the foundation of this project and the ongoing connection between China and these East African nations was laid in these conversations and secured in an agreement signed in 1966.

China's engagement with African countries was a bright spot in the context of the early 1960s. While resisting US imperialism was still seen as the primary contradiction by China, relations with the Soviet Union were an area of increasing concern. US aggression in Vietnam and its growing militarization of Japan, southern Korea, Taiwan, the Philippines, and Thailand, as well as its role in the bloody coup in Indonesia, all cast a shadow over China's efforts to pursue its course of socialist development and improve the lives of its people. The border war with India was a sad and frustrating deterioration of what had been an initial period of friendship in the 1950s. The ties of friendship and cooperation being forged with African lands would continue to be the better side of China's international situation, even as new challenges emerged in the coming decade, which will be explored in the next chapter.

CHAPTER 3: 1966–1976

The decade between 1966 and 1976 was one of continuing political contention over issues of socialist construction and over the relationship between the party and the masses. The Great Proletarian Cultural Revolution saw large-scale conflict in various parts of the country and had a significant impact on China's relations with other countries. Relations with the Soviet Union reached a low point in 1969 with military clashes on the border between the two socialist states. China's policies towards the United States took a dramatic turn as the Cultural Revolution ebbed in the early 1970s and the US war in Vietnam began to wind down. This period of PRC history concluded with the deaths of Zhou Enlai, Zhu De, and Mao Zedong in 1976, which set the stage for the resolution of internal party tensions and a major reorientation of developmental strategies. It was an era in which enemies became friends, and old friends became new enemies, a complex and often confusing phase of China's international relations.

As we have seen, relations between China and the Soviet Union, which had been so close in the 1950s, had deteriorated rapidly in the early '60s. The Soviets saw the Chinese as adventurists, ultraleftists pursuing a reckless course both in their domestic politics and in global affairs. The Chinese, on the other hand, viewed the Soviets as having betrayed the world revolution by compromising with the United States and as having followed a path of phony socialism in their own country. By August 1968, when the Soviets intervened in Czechoslovakia during a period of political unrest there, China, which had supported Soviet actions in Hungary in 1956, denounced the deployment of Red Army forces to Prague. Zhou Enlai, normally a voice of diplomatic restraint, made a public condemnation of the Soviets as "exactly the same as Hitler in the past in his aggression against Czechoslovakia, and as US imperialism today in its aggression against Vietnam." He further characterized the Soviet Union as "a country of social-imperialism and social-fascism." This was no longer a matter of principled debate over issues of socialist theory and practice among fraternal parties, but had become a stark power rivalry between these former close allies. This was a critical part of the overall devolution of what had been the socialist camp, the fragmentation of relations between the various socialist states, which created new opportunities for US imperialism to seek to split and weaken the development of socialism in the world.

It is important to recognize that China played a major role in the breakup of the socialist bloc. In characterizing the Soviet Union as "social imperialist," China was invoking the language of Lenin in 1914, denouncing the European social democrats, like Karl Kautsky, who had abandoned proletarian internationalism and supported the imperialist war being waged by the various national bourgeoisies. Lenin saw the social democrats as "socialists in words, but imperialists in deeds." By using this language against the Soviets, China was in fact exiting the socialist camp. This doesn't mean China was no longer a socialist country, but that they were no longer working with the other socialist states towards shared goals of world revolution.

The year 1969 saw the nadir of Sino-Soviet relations. The Nuclear Non-Proliferation Treaty signed by the United States, Britan, France, and the Soviet Union was seen by the Chinese, not without reason, as yet another attempt to maintain the monopoly on atomic weapons of the existing powers. China was not involved in these negotiations and was not a party to the treaty. Even more serious was the outbreak of actual armed clashes between Chinese and Soviet troops along their shared border, both in the east around islands in the Amur River and in Xinjiang. These violent confrontations took place just before the convening of the Ninth Party Congress which was meant to be a confirmation of the success of the Cultural Revolution and the reaffirmation of the leading role of the Communist Party in China. The threat of war with the Soviets hung over the Congress and sparked a campaign of preparations for a possible attack on the country's major cities.

The years of the Cultural Revolution from 1966 to early 1969 were a period where China was largely focused on domestic political struggles. The Foreign Ministry had recalled ambassadors from their posts, and many embassies and consulates around the world shut down as the conflicts within the party leadership intensified. In Beijing, Red Guards sought to enter the offices of the Foreign Ministry to search through records as part of the struggles against party officials. Zhou Enlai had to intervene personally at times to calm the scene and maintain the basic functions of international relations. Red Guards surrounded the embassies of the Soviet Union, France, and Indonesia, playing loud music and chanting slogans denouncing imperialism. The British legation in Beijing was attacked and partially burned in August 1967. Many countries closed or downsized their diplomatic presence.

Nonetheless, some international affairs were carefully maintained. Perhaps most importantly, China continued to provide assistance to Vietnam in its war with the United States. China sent material assistance, including anti-aircraft weapons, and supplied funds to sustain Vietnam's military. Even as relations with the Soviet Union worsened China continued to allow trains carrying aid to Vietnam from the Soviets to pass through Chinese territory. Solidarity with the Vietnamese overrode the tensions between the two largest socialist states. China also continued to support King Norodom Sihanouk in Cambodia, who had been a trusted friend for many years. In 1970, the Cambodian monarchy was overthrown by General Lon Nol, backed by the US, as the United States expanded its imperialist war into Cambodia and Laos. Sihanouk fled the country and was given refuge in Beijing. China also carried on its aid to friendly nations in Africa, including completing the construction of the Tanzam Railway, as mentioned above.

After the Ninth Party Congress in April 1969, the political landscape in China changed from one of widespread mass mobilization to one of renewed party leadership and the revived functioning of governmental institutions. The Revolutionary Committees, a new form of political organization which had emerged during the Cultural Revolution and brought together elements from the party, the army, and the masses, were gradually transformed into a system of party leadership with renewed ties and commitments to maintaining close links between the party and the masses. As part of the process, China began, slowly, to reopen diplomatic facilities in countries around the world. The party leadership also engaged, through 1969 and 1970, in a profound reassessment of the global political environment. The focus of this was a debate about the primary contradiction in China's relations with the wider world.

The question of the primary contradiction was based on the dialectical method of analyzing complex phenomena in order to determine which aspects of a process or situation were most important in determining the course of development. In any given state of affairs there could be many contradictions, but one would be predominant in shaping the dynamics of the future. For the Chinese, since liberation, the primary contradiction in world affairs had been that between the socialist world, most particularly China, and US imperialism. Given the history of Western domination and exploitation of China and the ongoing overt and covert acts of aggression carried on by the US, this had been an entirely correct assessment. Now, however, changing material realities might be bringing new contradictions to the fore.

On the one hand, US imperialism appeared to be in serious decline. The war in Vietnam was not going well. The Tet Offensive in 1968 had exposed the lies and failures of US military and political leaders. Millions of people in the United States were engaged in radical political movements against the war, for Black liberation, and for economic justice. The United States seemed more and more to be, as Mao Zedong had characterized it, a paper tiger. On the other hand, the Soviet Union was seen as an immediate and direct threat, especially in the wake of the border clashes of early 1969. The Soviet economy was growing, and the possibility of major armed conflict felt very real. Zhou Enlai's denunciation of the Soviets as "social-imperialists and social-fascists" was more than just a rhetorical flourish. It expressed the deep anxiety and growing antagonism among the Chinese leadership as their erstwhile ally became perhaps the most menacing enemy.

This was the context within which Mao Zedong and other leaders of the CPC undertook a thorough reevaluation of the dialectics of global affairs. Three dynamics were in play: relations between China and the Soviet Union, between China and the US, and between the United States and the Soviets. Mao came to the conclusion that in the current era, the primary contradiction had shifted to that between China and the Soviet Union. United States imperialism was under-

Ho Chi Minh. Photo: GL Archive/Alamy Stock Photo

stood as a spent force. This did not mean that China would undertake an effort to make an accommodation with the US, but it did set the stage for developments which were about to take place, driven on the US side by their own hopes of further dividing the socialist world in order to advance their interests in relation to the Soviets. While this new orientation, promoted by Mao Zedong, became the basis of

China's foreign policy in the early 1970s, not everyone was on board with the change of perspective.

Lin Biao was Minister of Defense and the main figure behind the initial compilation and circulation of the *Quotations from Chairman Mao Zedong*, the "little red book" which had become ubiquitous during the mass movements of the Cultural Revolution. Lin had been named in the CPC constitution adopted at the Ninth Party Congress as Mao's "close comrade-in-arms and successor." For reasons which have never been made entirely clear, Lin appears to have fundamentally disagreed with the revised understanding of the primary contradiction in world affairs that saw the Soviet Union as the greater threat to China than US imperialism. In what remains an obscure episode in the late summer of 1970, Lin tried to displace Mao and assume leadership of the party himself. This attempt failed, and Lin, along with members of his family, fled in a military aircraft, which then crashed in eastern Mongolia, killing everyone on board.

Even as these dramatic events were unfolding, the geopolitical landscape in China was shifting. The US had begun sending signals via diplomatic intermediaries that the Nixon administration was interested in improving relations with the People's Republic. In December 1969, the US ambassador to Poland told a Chinese delegation that Nixon wanted to have an "important and concrete conversation" with China's leaders. Over the following months, more behind-the-scenes exchanges took place between representatives of the two countries, mostly during social events in European or Asian capitals. The Chinese made it clear that the United States would have to change its position on Taiwan if there was to be any kind of progress in the overall relationship between the two sides. Edgar Snow, the US American journalist who had first written extensively about the Chinese revolution in the late 1930s and who had been a long-term friend of China, made a visit to Beijing in December 1970 and had a long interview with Chairman Mao. In their conversation, Mao commented that if the US president wanted to come to China, he would be welcome, so long as the US agreed to modify its policy towards the Taiwan question. Snow passed this message along, and other contacts through Romania and Pakistan echoed this position.

In March 1971, the first overt step in the process of opening relations with the United States took place when a ping-pong player on the US national team taking part in a tournament in Japan got into a friendly conversation with Chinese players. News of this reached Beijing, and the Chinese government extended an invitation to the US ping-pong team to come to China for some friendly matches with the Chinese team. In the games that followed, the Chinese diplomatically allowed the United States to win a couple of matches. This event became headline news in the US, the first positive coverage of China since liberation.

Through the rest of 1971, more backstage maneuvering took place, including secret visits by Kissinger to Beijing. In October 1971, the General Assembly of the United Nations voted to recognize the government of the People's Republic as the legitimate government of China—a move long overdue—and to have the PRC take the seat in the General Assembly and on the Security Council which had been held by the Nationalist remnants on Taiwan since 1949. Finally, in February 1972, Nixon flew to Beijing. In a gesture aimed at showing how the United States' attitude had changed, Nixon immediately shook Zhou Enlai's hand when he descended from his airplane, attempting to erase the insult directed at Zhou in Geneva in 1954 by John Foster Dulles. The United States was clearly seen as the side coming to China, as the side seeking to improve the relationship. Of course, this was part of the overall US strategy, trying to "play the China card" in order to antagonize the Soviets, but it also fit within the new Chinese sense of the primary contradiction. The Chinese reading of the state of US imperialism would prove to be overly optimistic, but for the moment, events seemed to be moving as Mao had anticipated.

Nixon stayed in China for two weeks, meeting with Mao and spending much more time with Zhou Enlai. After a week in Beijing, the US politicians shifted to Shanghai, and it was there that the final statement of the results of the discussion was made: the Shanghai Communique. This was a joint statement that set out the positions of the two sides and which became the basis for US policy in the following years. The most important provisions were that the United States recognized that Taiwan was part of China and that the issue of the relationship between Taiwan and the mainland was one which would be resolved by the Chinese people on both sides of the strait, without outside interference. The US agreed to reduce and eventually eliminate its military aid to Taiwan. These positions would be reaffirmed

US president Richard Nixon greeting Zhou Enlai in China, 1972. Photo: Byron Schumaker

with the formal establishment of full diplomatic relations in 1979 and in subsequent joint statements, though the United States never in fact accepted the reality of One China, and continue to interfere in China's internal affairs down to the present day.

Nonetheless, the opening of a less antagonistic relationship between China and the United States in 1972 had significant consequences for China's overall relations with the wider world. It was a factor in the US' decision to give up its imperialist war in Vietnam, though not until it had carried out the barbaric Christmas bombing raids on civilian targets in Hanoi in December 1972. It allowed China to begin to attract foreign investment from the capitalist world, beginning with Japan, which was sorely needed as China's split with the Soviet Union and many of the socialist states in Eastern Europe had cut off aid from those sources. But it also led to negative developments, as China sought to appease US concerns in areas which were not seen as vital to China. This was exemplified by China's recognition of the fascist Pinochet regime in Chile, which overthrew, with aid from the CIA, the democratically elected leftist government of Salvador Allende in September 1973.

The United States' opening of relations with China also allowed other Western powers to recognize the PRC, or to upgrade existing relations to full ambassadorial level. Britain, which had recognized China in the 1950s but only maintained consular-level ties, agreed to the full formal exchange of ambassadors. China recognized the West German government, an act which it had previously refused to do in solidarity with the German Democratic Republic, and Bonn sent an ambassador to Beijing. Perhaps most importantly, China and Japan established formal diplomatic relations. The two countries had maintained extensive cultural and social contacts, but serious issues around Taiwan and the legacy of Japanese imperialist aggression and invasion, as well as Japan's position as a bastion of US imperialist forces after 1945, had prevented governmental relations. In the new environment following the Nixon visit, China and Japan were able to resolve, or in some instances gloss over, these issues in order to establish formal links, which facilitated Japanese investment in China as well.

While the opening of relations with the US and expanding ties and engagements with other countries in the capitalist world was becoming the new orientation of China's international posture, political conflicts within the CPC leadership persisted in the mid-1970s. Figures such as Deng Xiaoping, who had been severely criticized during the mass movement period of the Cultural Revolution, reemerged to play important roles in both domestic policy and foreign affairs. Deng gave a major speech at a special session of the UN General Assembly in April 1974 in which he laid out China's perspective on the geopolitical state of play, denouncing both the United States and the Soviet Union as "superpowers" seeking global hegemony, and reiterating China's basic principles of peaceful coexistence. Deng also elaborated on the model of "three worlds," with the US and Soviets as the First World, the developing countries of Asia, Africa, and Latin American constituted the Third World, and the developed countries "between the two" making up the Second World. China considered itself part of the Third World, and supported global revolutionary transformation.

While China was stepping into a new role at the UN and in its new connections with countries in all three of the "worlds" Deng described, a political grouping centered around Jiang Qing (the wife of Mao Zedong), Yao Wenyuan, Zhang Chunqiao, and Wang Hongwen continued to raise issues of the bureaucratization of the party and fears of a capitalist restoration. It viewed Deng and other cadres who had returned to official duties in the post–Ninth Party Congress era as rightists who still needed to be struggled against. Mao himself did not act decisively to settle these tensions, and as his health deteriorated in the mid-1970s, and as Zhou Enlai also faced increasingly serious health issues in these years, China remained in a limbo state in many ways. This situation was only to be resolved with the dramatic events of 1976.

Zhou Enlai died of cancer on January 8 in the Number 305 Hospital of the People's Liberation Army. Tensions between Zhou and the leftist grouping around Jiang Qing had been growing over the previous two years, and they welcomed his passing. But in April, at the time of the Qingming Festival when people swept the graves of their ancestors, a large demonstration developed at the Monument to the People's Heroes in Tiananmen Square to commemorate Zhou. This was viewed as a counterrevolutionary movement by the leftists and was broken up by the police, highlighting the lingering animosities within the party leadership. Zhu De, considered the founder of the Red Army in the late 1920s and known as a highly respected party elder, died on July 6. Three weeks later, northern China was shaken by the Tangshan earthquake, centered about ninety-three miles east of Beijing, which killed around three hundred thousand people and caused widespread damage, even in the capital. This was viewed by many people, in line with Chinese traditional beliefs, as an omen of great changes taking place.

On September 9, Chairman Mao Zedong died. This was a momentous event in the history of modern China and the People's Republic, opening a political space for the resolution of the deep and long-running contradictions within the leadership of the Communist Party. This would lead to dramatic transformations in both domestic economic development and in China's relations with the rest of the world, especially the global capitalist order centered on the United States. These changes, and the evolving context of world geopolitical dynamics, will be the focus of the next chapters.

PART TWO

CHAPTER 4: 1976–1989

The period immediately after the death of Mao Zedong in September 1976 was one of great transition within the Communist Party of China and of continuing turbulence in many parts of the world, which often involved China in one way or another. United States imperialism continued to appear to be a spent force, which seemed to confirm the reassessment of the primary contradiction in China's relations with the rest of the world. China saw the Soviet Union as its principal adversary, and this shaped the conduct of foreign relations for the People's Republic, often in ways which were problematic for the overall situation of global socialism.

In October 1976, the four members of what was referred to as the "Gang of Four," Jiang Qing, Yao Wenyuan, Zhang Chunqiao, and Wang Hongwen, were arrested by security forces and charged with various anti-party offenses. This was the overt beginning of a long period of internal debate and discussion: about the state of the country, the lessons to be drawn from the previous decades of struggle, and the path forward to be taken in the pursuit of socialist construction. The two years between October 1976 and November 1978 saw the Chinese leadership mainly engaged in this internal effort to end the long period of conflict among the leadership and to determine a new direction for the future. China had made great advances in many areas, including agricultural production, the development of a modern industrial sector, and the provision of basic social services. But the country remained poor, as population growth had absorbed much of the increase in production, and industrial policy remained focused on heavy industry rather than consumer goods. China had attained a kind of egalitarianism of poverty. But Deng Xiaoping and others argued that this was not socialism. Socialism is to be a society of prosperity, in which those who labor to produce value share equitably in the distribution of the fruits of their labor. People should live well, with more than just a sufficiency of material goods. To attain this, China needed to find a way to expand production much more rapidly and thoroughly than they had been doing. This is the logic that led to the program of reform and opening.

The essence of the reform policy was the use of the mechanisms of the market to develop the productive economy. This required access to both capital and modern technologies and information, which could best be acquired from the capitalist world. The adoption of the program of "reform and opening," announced at a plenum of the party leadership in November 1978, which also saw the reemergence of Deng Xiaoping as the key figure in the leadership of the CPC and the government, would dramatically reshape China's international relations in the years to come. But during the period of internal debate leading to this transformation in China's path towards socialism, there were several serious developments in global affairs and China's relationships which unfolded while domestic politics dominated the leadership's attention. Zhou Enlai, who had long guided China's foreign policy administration, had died in January 1976, and the Foreign Ministry and diplomatic service were more or less running on autopilot during these years.

Perhaps the most dramatic developments in the late 1970s took place in Southeast Asia. The United States had been defeated in Vietnam. US forces left the country in 1973, and in April 1975, the country was reunified with the victory of the National Liberation Front in the south. In Cambodia, the Khmer Rouge came to power in 1975 and embarked on their radical program of social transformation, which soon became a violent program of forced relocation and ruralization in which many people perished. The Khmer Rouge also carried out harsh actions aimed at the ethnic Vietnamese communities in the eastern part of the country.

During the war in Vietnam, the communist forces there and the government in northern Vietnam had received support and material assistance from both the Soviet Union and China, but as the war ended and Vietnam embarked on new programs of development in the wake of reunification, the country became more closely allied with the Soviets. In Cambodia, the long-established ties with China continued. In the context of the antagonism between China and the Soviet Union, these relationships contributed to deepening tensions between Vietnam and Cambodia, which resulted in the invasion of Cambodia by Vietnam in 1978 and the overthrow of the Khmer Rouge government. This in turn led to the invasion of Vietnam by China in February and March 1979. This was described by the Chinese as "teaching Vietnam a lesson" and was a limited incursion. Chinese forces withdrew after a month of fighting in which the battle-hardened Vietnamese forces generally gained the upper hand. The spectacle of these conflicts, first between Vietnam and Cambodia and then China and Vietnam, was deeply unsettling for many on the left worldwide. The fragmentation of the socialist camp which had begun with the Sino-Soviet split in 1959 had reached a point where socialist countries were going to war with each other. China had played a major role in this process.

China's perception of the Soviet Union as a "social imperialist" country shaped its conduct in other areas as well. In Angola and Mozambique, where the Soviets had supplied aid to the national liberation struggle against the Portuguese colonialists, China adopted a position opposing the Soviet-backed movement and aligned its policy with that of the United States. The communist victories in Indochina, Ethiopia, Afghanistan, and elsewhere; the faltering of the US economy in the 1970s; and the beginnings of China's opening to the capitalist world in search of investment and other resources for its development, even before the launching of the program of reform and opening—all seemed to validate the belief that US imperialism was waning. This belief led China to an effective accommodation with the United States in at least some aspects of global affairs.

This new relationship of accommodation with US imperialism was illustrated with some theatricality by Deng Xiaoping's visit to the United States in January and February 1979. He was hosted for a state dinner at the White House by President Jimmy Carter; visited Atlanta, Georgia, where he toured the headquarters of Coca-Cola; and was photographed wearing a cowboy hat during a stop in Texas. This was a honeymoon period in US-China relations. At the same time, just as China was embarking on its project of reform and opening, profound

Deng Xiaoping dons a cowboy hat while attending a rodeo in Texas, 1979. Photo: Scott Mc Kiernan

changes were brewing in the West which would lead to a new phase of revival for US imperialism. The 1970s, in the United States and many other advanced industrial economies, was a period both of continuing decline in the profitability of productive economic activities and of increasing anxiety about the successes of communist and other leftist movements and governments around the world.

In January 1979, right before Deng's visit to the US, an open letter to President Carter called for taking a harder line against the Soviet Union, against socialist and communist advances, and for the remilitarization of the United States. It was signed by 170 retired generals and admirals, among others, and specifically attacked "Soviet imperialism," including China as a country threatened by the Soviets. This was a prelude to the election of Ronald Reagan in 1980 and his embrace of neoliberalism, which resulted in the major reorientation of US political life, both domestically and internationally. Reagan sought to finally end the Cold War by driving the Soviet Union to bankruptcy through a new arms race. His pursuit of this objective took the United States from being the largest creditor nation in the world to the largest debtor nation as he poured hundreds of billions of dollars into new arms systems, many of which never worked, but which forced the Soviet leadership to divert critical resources from domestic uses to expanding their own military capabilities. This, in tandem with the failed Soviet intervention in Afghanistan, became critical elements in the process of decline and collapse of the socialist system in the USSR. As this was taking place through the 1980s, China was charting its own new path of socialist construction.

China's relations with the United States continued to develop in a basically positive way. US investment began to flow into China, with joint ventures and other productive enterprises ramping up in the Special Economic Zones (SEZs) set aside for foreign corporations. In those zones, they were exempt from some Chinese rules and regulations, and a share of profits could be repatriated to the West. As this process got underway, US politicians, media pundits, and some academics began to anticipate that China would, as it liberalized its economy, inevitably undergo a political transformation. Western capitalist ideology associated markets with democracy, the kind of bourgeois democracy which allowed capitalist elites to maintain their power through the domination of electoral politics by money. Their hope and expectation was that, at some point in the future, the rule of the Communist Party would be replaced by some kind of new political system which would be fully integrated with and subordinate to the global capitalist system dominated by the United States. This belief, this hope for a future of ever-greater power and hegemonic leadership by the United States, would persist, despite some setbacks and frustrations, for the next three decades.

As the process of reform began in the early 1980s, China's engagement with global capitalism did indeed grow and deepen. One major way in which we can see this is by considering a series of conferences and other discussion about how reform should proceed. How fast should policies be changed? What kinds of changes should be made first? In confronting basic questions about reform, Chinese leaders sought the advice of business leaders, economists, and government officials from the US and other capitalist states, as well as consulted with officials from some of the Eastern European socialist states that had been experimenting with liberalizing their economies. Isabella Weber has written a wonderful book, *How China Escaped Shock Therapy*, that discusses these meetings and the ideas about reform which were debated. Not surprisingly, many of the Western capitalist consultants advocated rapid, all-out reform, the kind of "shock therapy" which would later devastate the economy and society of what became the "former Soviet Union." Some members of the Chinese leadership, such as Hu Yaobang and Zhao Ziyang, leaned towards this approach. Others, however, such as Chen Yun and An Zhiwen, cautioned against too rapid or too sweeping a program. Many of the Chinese participants in these reform debates drew both on Marxist theory and experience in the twentieth century and on China's own history of political economic theory and practice.

One key question which arose in these debates became central to the reform process in the 1980s was price reform. The use of markets to develop the productive economy made market prices an important mechanism for the allocation of resources. But shifting from a system in which prices were largely set by government planners to one in which prices would be allowed to move according to market signals was a major change. Advocates of all-out reform called for simply freeing prices all at once, while others wanted to pursue a more incremental price liberalization in order to buffer the effects of rising prices on consumers. An initial effort to drop price regulations in 1986 led to severe impacts on many citizens, and was reversed after a few weeks. But the promoters of rapid reform persisted, and in 1988, prices were deregulated once again. The results of this, which included sharp rises in commodities needed by many urban households, contributed directly to the social unrest which began to arise in the spring of 1989, to which we will return shortly.

The first decade of reform in China was also a period of political change in the Soviet Union. The renewed hostility towards the Soviets on the part of the Reagan administration was carried forward in a two-faced manner. Military spending in the United States was dramatically increased, with flashy weapons systems like the "Star Wars" laser technologies being touted as shifting the strategic advantage in favor of the United States. At the same time, Reagan seemed to embrace the liberalizing reform leaders, primarily Mikhail Gorbachev who came to power in Moscow in the mid-1980s. Gorbachev pursued policies of *glasnost* and *perestroika*, releasing political tensions in the Eastern European socialist states as well as in the Soviet Union itself. The new arms race with the United States and the Soviet intervention in Afghanistan, in support of an elected socialist government there that was under attack by US-funded jihadist groups, drained resources from the mainstream economy and undermined the standard of living of ordinary Soviet citizens. By 1989, social unrest in Eastern Europe was reaching crisis dimensions.

In China, contradictions emerged in the first decade of reform and opening. This included corruption among officials in the government and Communist Party cadres, the dislocation of labor as state enterprises were put on new managerial systems to streamline their operations and make them function along market-oriented lines, and growing inequality as some parts of society benefitted from the reforms more quickly than others. These contradictions also gave rise to social unrest. In Beijing and other cities, students and some young professionals who felt themselves being left behind by the course of reform began to agitate for greater input into the policy-making process. Their sense of frustration was intensified in April when Hu Yaobang, who had been an advocate of rapid reform and who had strong links to youth organizations, died of a heart attack. Students in the capital organized demonstrations in honor of Hu, which became forums for expressing their discontent with the pace of reform. An editorial in the *People's Daily* characterized the student demonstrations as unpatriotic and anti-socialist. This further upset many young people, and the demonstrations first grew larger, and then morphed into the occupation of Tiananmen Square, at the center of Beijing, shutting down the National Museum and disrupting normal activities in the heart of the city.

As China had been pursuing the first decade of its reforms and the Soviet leadership under Gorbachev had been initiating the policies of *glasnost* and *perestroika*, relations between the Soviet Union and China had eased, and by the late 1980s it seemed that more positive and constructive links between the two countries could be resumed. A visit to Beijing by Gorbachev was planned for May 1989, and it was hoped that this would lead to closer ties. The Chinese were eager to show the Soviets and the wider world the gains they had made through their reform efforts. Foreign media came to China in large numbers as the date of Gorbachev's visit approached, including US television and newspaper reporters. The occupation of Tiananmen Square became a major focus of the Western press, which eagerly portrayed it as heralding the impending collapse of the communist government.

While the unrest developing in the spring of 1989 was portrayed as a broad-based movement for "democracy," in reality it was an entirely urban-centered effort to reshape government policies in the interest of some specific social groupings, mostly university students and young professionals. The protests had little impact in rural areas where the majority of Chinese still lived, nor in more than a handful of urban centers. Most of the initial participants were solidly in support of the socialist system. It was only over the passing of several weeks in late April and early May that the situation changed in negative ways.

The occupation, which had grown out of initially legitimate concerns on the part of some students and young professionals, came to be taken over by elements opposed to the socialist system. Attempts to open negotiations between the dominant leaders of the occupation and the government were rebuffed by the demonstrators, or turned into opportunities to promote their own agenda. Wu'er Kaixi, one of the most radical occupiers, showed up for a meeting with leaders of the government and the CPC wearing his pajamas, a gesture of contempt and disrespect which did nothing to advance serious efforts to resolve the situation. When Gorbachev arrived in Beijing in mid-May, the normal welcoming events for a state visitor had to be canceled and he was taken into the Great Hall of the People, on the west side of Tiananmen Square, by a side door, further humiliating the Chinese leaders. Meanwhile the international bourgeois media, most prominently the US television broadcaster Dan Rather, gleefully predicted the imminent fall of the PRC government and its replacement by a "democratic" regime which would be fully subordinate to US interests. After a brief stay in Beijing, Gorbachev returned to Moscow. The occupation of Tiananmen Square continued through the end of May and into the beginning of June.

Given the intransigence of the leadership of the occupation, some of whom openly called for overthrowing the government and spoke of the need for blood to flow in the streets, state and party leaders finally resolved on clearing the square and the need to restore normal functioning to the center of Beijing, the nation's capital. When units of the People's Liberation Army began to move into the city, they were attacked by violent elements in the streets, primarily on the west side along Chang'an Avenue. Trucks were stopped and burned, weapons were seized from troops who been ordered to act with extreme restraint, and in the ensuing fighting, several hundred people were killed, including nearly three hundred soldiers. By around 2:00

a.m., the PLA units had reached Tiananmen Square, where only a small number of individuals remained. The square was encircled, with an opening left at the southeast corner so that those who wished to depart could do so, which most of the remaining occupiers chose to do. Only a few individuals were arrested that night, and no one was killed in Tiananmen Square, a fact which was reported at the time by eyewitnesses, including some Western reporters.

Almost immediately these events were portrayed by the mainstream media in the West, especially in the United States, as the "Tiananmen massacre." China was subjected to widespread condemnation by Western politicians and by the news media. Over the following months, contact between China and the West was drastically curtailed. Tourism and study abroad programs ceased almost entirely. China was seen as a pariah state in Western elite circles. The occupation of Tiananmen Square, as it increasingly transformed into an anti-government movement aimed at changing the political system in China and turning the country into a compliant cog in the machinery of global capitalism, had raised the hopes of US corporate and political elites, whose faith in the proposition that economic reform would automatically lead to political transformation, seemed to be being rewarded. The determination of the Chinese leadership to restore order and to maintain the project of socialist construction frustrated those hopes, and for a while, this led to China's isolation from the main capitalist states.

The events of April to June also raised serious questions about the nature and pace of reform for the party leadership. The effects of price deregulation in 1986 and especially in 1988 had been the initial trigger for social unrest. Some elements in the leadership felt that the reform program needed to be cut back, if not reversed. Others, including Deng Xiaoping, saw the need to advance with greater caution, but were determined to persist in the overall project. Leaders like Zhao Ziyang who had supported rapid reform and who had encouraged the demonstrations in Tiananmen Square, lost their positions and were replaced with figures like Jiang Zemin who were aligned with Deng's commitment to continuing reform. China's isolation would persist for the next couple of years, and during this time renewed debates over the reform policies continued as the Chinese leadership sought to fine-tune the next phase of its project.

In the months following the resolution of the Tiananmen crisis, events in Eastern Europe took a very different course. This shift would reshape the wider European order and become part of a capitalist expansion into formerly socialist realms, with often disastrous results for the lives of ordinary people. The Chinese leaders followed these developments closely and understood the importance of maintaining the path they had chosen. In August 1989, the border between Hungary and Austria was opened, setting off a period when many people crossed into the West from the Eastern European socialist states, which had been suffering from the effects of Reagan's new arms race with the Soviets. People from Poland and the German Democratic Republic made their way to Hungary via Czechoslovakia, where the government allowed this traffic to flow through without impediment. As the autumn of 1989 advanced, political crises in many of the Eastern European countries deepened, leading to the opening of the border between East and West Berlin in November and to the collapse of socialist governments across the region. Despite the fact that China had played a major role in the fragmentation of the socialist camp in the 1960s and 1970s, the disappearance of these states was seen as a major defeat for the global socialist project. The Soviet Union would survive for two more years, but the effects of Reagan's policies and the costs of the Soviet military activities in Afghanistan, along with Gorbachev's abandonment of effective leadership of the Communist Party, eventually resulted in the collapse of the Soviet Union in 1991.

As China entered the second decade of the reform era, it faced serious challenges and a rapidly changing international environment. The decline and fall of the socialist states in Eastern Europe and the Soviet Union fundamentally changed the geopolitical logic which had shaped Chinese foreign policy since the late 1960s. US imperialism was resurgent under the neoliberal regime of the Reagan and Bush administrations. The gains which had been made in the first years of reform had been significant, but far from sufficient in fulfilling China's needs for enhancing the livelihoods of its people and moving towards an initial stage of socialism by developing its productive economy. As the 1990s began, China's leaders had to make careful choices about their next moves; the way forward was fraught and complex. How they addressed these challenges will be considered in the next chapter.

CHAPTER 5: 1990–2010

China remained the target of criticism from the Western capitalist states for the first two years of the 1990s. There was widespread condemnation of the resolution of the Tiananmen crisis, the suppression of what had become an attempted counterrevolution to overthrow the government of the People's Republic and replace it with a new regime friendly to and compliant with the interests of the US-led global capitalist system. This did not mean that the US and other Western corporations ceased their operations in China. They were making good profits from the labor of Chinese workers, and this also allowed them, as part of the overall neoliberal reorientation of the US and European economies, to put downward pressure on wages and move against trade unions. The demonization of China in the media and by politicians may even have served to try to put pressure on the government there to grant greater concessions and make further accommodations with the imperialists.

The beginning of the '90s was a period of debate within the Communist Party over the future course of reform. In the wake of the unrest of 1989, some called the whole project into question, but in the end the leadership understood that China needed to follow through on the path of development through the use of market mechanisms if they truly wanted to grow the economy and reach a level of material prosperity which would enable them to implement social distribution of accumulated wealth. They resolved to persevere, but to pursue the path of reform with caution and ensure the overall leadership of the party as the key to the long-term success of the project. The class nature of the system needed to be preserved, and the Communist Party was the only means of ensuring that would be the case.

From January 18 to February 21, 1992, Deng Xiaoping made a tour of several of the Special Economic Zones along the coast in Guangdong province. This was referred to in the Chinese press as a *nanxun* [南巡], a term which originally referred to the visits to southern China by the Kangxi and Qianlong emperors in the seventeenth and eighteenth centuries. The historical significance of the term was meant to indicate the seriousness and importance of the tour. During these visits, Deng made repeated statements about the need to go forward with the program of reform and opening. He was communicating to the Chinese people the resolution and determination of the party and the government to stay the course and carry through the project. He was also, importantly, sending a signal to the Western capitalist states that China was committed to maintaining its policies of openness to foreign investment. The Chinese leadership well understood that they had to continue to attract investment, technology, and other knowledge from the global capitalist system in order to build the kind of modern, efficient, and productive economy the country needed to prosper.

Deng's southern tour proved to be effective in convincing US and other Western business leaders to renew and expand their engagement with China. This was a moment of political transition in the United States, as the Democratic Clinton administration was replacing the twelve-year-long rule of the Republicans. The Reagan and Bush years had shifted the overall parameters of US politics, and Clinton was far from being a left-liberal figure, but the change in the presidency was seen as a moment of opportunity, including the chance to reset the relationship with China. Even before Deng's *nanxun*, in 1990, China had tried to signal its wish to work with the West and its willingness to make concessions and accommodations. In 1990, as a political gesture, the anti-party dissident Fang Lizhi was allowed to depart the country after entering the US embassy in Beijing. That same year, China abstained from voting against the resolution in the United Nations authorizing the US invasion of Iraq from Kuwait. These actions did not yield immediate results, but they set a precedent for a future resumption of more normal diplomatic relations. In the wake of Deng's reinvigoration of the reform program, this is just how things developed.

This did not go forward without some further bumps in the road. In July 1993, US Navy ships detained a Chinese freighter and accused China of shipping chemical weapons components to Iran. After twenty-four days, the Chinese allowed inspectors to search the vessel, where no such items were found. Despite this heavy-handed demonstration of imperialist arrogance, Jiang Zemin, who had become China's main leader after 1989, attended the first summit meeting of the Asia-Pacific Economic Cooperation group in Seattle in November 1993, where he met with President Clinton. Subsequently, Clinton lifted some sanctions on China and restored most-favored-nation trading status to the country, without imposing special conditions. In 1997 and 1998, Jiang and Clinton made recip-rocal state visits and signed further agreements to promote expand-ing trade and framing the relationship between the countries as one of "strategic partnership."

A critical factor in the warming of relations between China and the US and other Western countries was the adoption by China of a posture of accommodation with global capitalism. Deng Xiaoping proposed a set of guidelines for China's leaders to follow. Central to his view was the need to "bide [our] time to build [our] capacities" [*taoguang yanghui* 韜光養晦] and to "be good at maintaining a low profile" [*shan yu shouzhuo* 善于守拙]. In other words, to allow the US to believe they were running the show, to let them continue to hope for a political transition in China, while they provided the invest-ment, technologies, and other assistance China needed to advance its program of socialist construction, without emphasizing it. China never abandoned or retreated from its goal of building a socialist economy and society. But they chose to make accommodations with capitalism and imperialism in order to gain the things they needed. This posture prevailed from the early 1990s until the second decade of the twenty-first century.

The late 1990s was a period during which China experienced triumph and tragedy while steadily advancing along its chosen path. In July 1997, after a decade of negotiations with Great Britain, the Peo-ple's Republic reassumed sovereignty over Hong Kong. Seized by the British during the First Opium War in 1839–1842, Hong Kong island had been claimed as a colony in the Treaty of Nanjing that ended the war and became the first of the Unequal Treaties that framed the dom-

Jiang Zemin shakes hand with Prince Charles at the ceremony where Hong Kong is returned to China. Photo: South China Morning Post/Robert Ng

ination of China by Western imperialism and launched the Century of Humiliation. Chinese residents of Hong Kong had never held any democratic rights under the British. They were denied any kind of participation in the formulation of the policies which regulated their lives. The British even brought in colonial subjects from other parts of their empire, especially Ghurkhas from India and Nepal, to serve as police officers. The governor of the colony was always a white male, appointed by the government in London. The settlement at Kowloon, on the mainland across from Hong Kong Island, was added a few years later, and in 1897, an additional land grab of the New Territories completed the formation of the colony. In 1949, as China was being liberated by the People's Liberation Army, the Chinese leaders decided not to invade the British colony or the smaller Portuguese enclave at Macao, though both could have been easily taken. As China began to return to a significant role in world affairs, the time seemed right to finally reassert sovereignty over all of the territories occupied by the imperialists. Hong Kong was recovered in 1997, and Macao followed in 1999 after 440 years as a foreign possession.

The process of bringing British colonial rule to an end and reintegrating Hong Kong with the rest of the country entailed a complex process of diplomacy which began in the mid-1980s. China exercised great self-restraint through the years of negotiation, which finally led to an agreement that the British would depart, and that Hong Kong would become a Special Administrative Region (SAR) of China and once again be recognized as an integral part of the People's Republic. This agreement was embodied in what is known as the Basic Law, which functions as a kind of constitution for Hong Kong, and stipulated that the Basic Law would remain in place for fifty years, until 2047, though it would be subject to amendment through a legislative process. Unlike when Chinese residents in Hong Kong had been deprived of democratic rights under the British, the Basic Law set out a process for developing democratic institutions, including the Legislative Council. China adopted a policy of "One Country, Two Systems" which recognized that Hong Kong would retain a distinctive legal and political system during the five decades of the Basic Law, and perhaps beyond. This policy is also applied in Macao and would be the basis for reunification with Taiwan when that finally came about. Under the Basic Law, Hong Kong developed a lively multiparty electoral system, different from the money-driven bourgeois democracies of the West, and more like those of other post-colonial states in Southeast Asia, like Indonesia or Malaysia.

The year 1997 was also the year of the Asian financial crisis, in which China's resumption of sovereignty over Hong Kong came to play an important part. The crisis began when exchange rate speculators in the international money markets, seeking to exploit tiny differences in the valuation of different national currencies by either betting on a rise or a fall in the value of a given currency, targeted the currency of Thailand, the *baht*. Their maneuvers drove the *baht* into a sharp decline, seriously disrupting the Thai economy and causing hardship to many ordinary people who saw the value of their savings drop dramatically. The attack on the *baht* had a ripple effect on other monetary systems, especially in Southeast Asia, where the economies of many countries were closely interlinked. Indonesia saw a rapid collapse in the value of its currency, and Malaysia also suffered from the depredations of speculators. The Philippines were next on the list, and by late in the year, even the South Korean *won* faced serious problems due to the activities of the speculators. This was a very serious crisis, affecting countries all across East and Southeast Asia.

The other major currency in the regional money markets was the Hong Kong dollar. Hong Kong was a center of financial activity as well as commercial and manufacturing operations. The Hong Kong dollar had long been regarded as one of the most stable currencies in the world and thus was attractive to economic actors around the region and beyond. This made it potentially a great target for the speculators, who launched attacks on the money markets in Hong Kong and elsewhere. At this point the central government in Beijing intervened. China had accumulated significant amount of foreign exchange reserves, especially US dollars, Japanese *yen*, and Hong Kong dollars. The People's Bank of China was able to inject massive amounts of money into the Hong Kong financial system to support the value of the dollar, and frustrate the greed of the speculators. These actions not only protected the value of the Hong Kong dollar, but also ensured that the economy of the city was not disrupted, the people did not suffer, and the links between Hong Kong and the rest of the Chinese economy were not disrupted. This helped to bring the Asian financial crisis to an end. China's ability to do this was due in large degree to its socialist system: the party and government had the capacity to deploy the wealth accumulated in the course of the reform policies as social assets, protecting the livelihoods of the people and the sovereignty and stability of the country.

China's performance during the Asian financial crisis and the return of Hong Kong were great successes for the People's Republic. China was recognized as an important country which needed to be taken seriously. But US imperialism continued to see China as an opportunity for exploitation, an arena within which its corporations could extract value from the labor of Chinese workers, and persevered in their hope and expectation that China could be led along a path which would end with the abandonment of socialism and the country's complete integration into the global capitalist system. The niceties of diplomatic language and gestures of mutual respect performed during the exchanges of state visits masked an attitude of contempt and the steady pursuit of the goals of subordinating China to the interests of capital.

United States imperialism was of course active on many fronts in the late 1990s. The collapse of the socialist states in Eastern Europe and the breakup of the Soviet Union had opened new horizons for

Chinese embassy bombed by US warplanes in Belgrade, 1999. Photo: Karl Blanchet

capitalism with the fire sale of social assets, putting the wealth which had been built up by the labor of working people into the hands of private corporations, many of them from the United States or other Western countries. The US was dedicated to eradicating any vestiges of socialism in Europe, and in 1999, it was engaged in a war to destroy the Yugoslav Republic, the last of the socialist states, breaking it up into several small successor regimes. On May 7, US warplanes bombed the Chinese embassy there during an air assault on Belgrade, killing three journalists working in the building. The CIA, which had been responsible for this air action, claimed that it had misidentified the site and given the attacking aircraft the wrong coordinates. This was seen as a flimsy excuse, and large demonstrations took place outside US diplomatic offices in Beijing and other cities around China to protest the bombing. The Belgrade attack was not the only instance when US military and espionage activities clashed with China's security. Less than a year later, a US spy plane flying off the China coast collided with a Chinese PLA aircraft defending the country's airspace, and the US plane had to land on Hainan Island. China repatriated the crew, but the incident further exposed the reality of imperialist aggression towards China.

The Belgrade bombing and the spy plane incident took place while China and the United States were conducting an elaborate set of negotiations aimed at offering China membership in the World Trade Organization (WTO). The WTO is the main international institution for managing trade relations among the capitalist economies. The US wanted China to join in order to have them be subject to the rules and regulations administered by the WTO. Disputes over tariffs or other issues in economic exchanges between member states were also to be resolved through a process of negotiation and arbitration. From the US perspective, bringing China into the WTO would cement the country's place as a component of the global capitalist system, further advancing their hopes for an eventual political transition in China to a fully bourgeois government aligned with US interests.

For China, the question of joining the WTO had other implications. The project of reform and opening was aimed at bringing investment and state-of-the-art productive technologies to help develop the country's economy and give China the ability to pursue its goals of socialist construction. While investment by US corporations had been flowing into China since the 1980s, the Jackson–Vanick Amendment of 1974, which had made it illegal for US businesses to share or trade in certain technologies with either the Soviet Union or China, still imposed restrictions on China's access to cutting-edge tech. Membership in the WTO would render these restrictions void. In the wake of the Belgrade bombing, China had been able to extract some concessions from the US in the negotiations over the terms of China's admittance, but China also had to give ground on various issues which would be beneficial to Western interests. In many ways, the decision to pursue membership in the WTO was the ultimate expression of the posture of accommodation with global capitalism that characterized China's international relations between the 1990s and 2010. Leaders in the Communist Party and the PRC government felt that the compromises and concessions they had to make would ultimately be worthwhile as China accomplished its goals of modernization and economic development. They were determined to maintain the leading role of the CPC as the guarantor of the socialist project, overseeing the activities of private capital in the country and working to buffer the negative effects, the contradictions, which they understood would arise in the course of reform. The talks with the US carried into 2000 but finally yielded an agreement. China formally entered the WTO in December 2001, three months after the attacks on the World Trade Center in New York and the Pentagon in Washington, DC, had set off a profound reorientation of US international activities.

The administration of George W. Bush saw the attacks of September 11 not only as a chance to act against the jihadist groups which had carried them out, but as an opportunity to initiate a wider campaign to dominate the Muslim nations of the Middle East and the oil resources located there. The "War on Terror" quickly became the primary focus of the United States' policy, with the US deploying troops to Afghanistan by the end of 2001 and preparing the for invasion of Iraq—which had no connection to the September 11, 2001 events—in March 2003. These wars, which did tremendous damage to the lives of ordinary people across the region and spilled over into Syria and East Africa, would drag on for years, accomplishing little beyond the devastation of economic and social life for millions of Muslims with no relation to the purported objective of fighting fundamentalist terrorism.

The early years of the "War on Terror" gave rise to an unusual convergence of interests between the United States and China. Radical jihadist elements in the Xinjiang Uighur Autonomous Region of western China, who sought to break the area away from the People's Republic and establish a fundamentalist Islamic state called East Turkestan, had been waging a sometimes-violent struggle against the Chinese government. Terrorist bombings had taken place not only in Xinjiang but in Beijing and other cities, along with knife attacks on travelers at railway station in places like Kunming. China agreed to allow the US to establish intelligence gathering stations near the border with Afghanistan. The US, in turn, designated the radical jihadist separatist movements of the East Turkestan Liberation Organization and the East Turkestan Islamic Movement as terrorist groups.

The "War on Terror" became the dominant concern of US policy in the rest of the Bush administration and into the Obama years. As the US deployed massive military and economic resources to the Middle East, China receded from the consciousness of foreign policy elites. The first decade of the twenty-first century saw China's economy continue the rapid growth which had begun with the resumption of reform after Deng Xiaoping's southern tour in 1992. Annual growth in gross domestic product (GDP), the basic measure of the production of goods and services in an economy, was near and often over 10 percent from 1997 to 2010, peaking at 14.2 percent in 2007. This was an unprecedented level of sustained growth in a major economy. While the US was devoted to war and destruction during these years, China was making great strides towards its goals of developing its productive economy.

Deng Xiaoping had died in 1997, and a succession of leaders followed into the early 2000s, including Jiang Zemin and Hu Jintao who carried on the posture of biding time and building capabilities. These leaders put forward certain slogans to characterize their policies and China's position in the world. They emphasized China's objectives of improving the lives of the Chinese people and the idea that China's rise was not something which other countries needed to be concerned about. China was following a "peaceful rise" into a "harmonious world." These messages were largely intended to reassure the United States, who in any case was focused on their military adventures in Afghanistan, Iraq, and elsewhere. China continued along its path of socialist development, but quietly and without challenging US leadership in the capitalist world.

While the relationship between China and the United States was certainly the primary dynamic in the foreign policy of the PRC, it was by no means the only international activity for the country. China was eager to improve its links with its immediate neighbors. As early as 1988, an agreement was reached with Mongolia to settle lingering border issues. The border with Russia, which had been the site of military conflict in 1969, was not as easily settled, but as the relationship with Russia steadily improved, a process inaugurated by the visit of Boris Yeltsin to China in 1992, the eastern section of the border was delimited in 1997, and in 2008 a treaty finally settled all remaining issues. The relationship with Russia would continue to evolve, as will be discussed later.

Another important area in which China was engaged was Southeast Asia. Relations in this region had begun to improve with the settlement of border issues with Vietnam in 1991. Vietnam had embarked on its own program of economic reform, in many ways emulating the Chinese model, and the two countries managed to put the clashes of the late 1970s behind them. In 1990, China was able to restore normal diplomatic relations with Indonesia and exchanged ambassadors with Singapore for the first time. China's role in restabilizing monetary markets in 1997 was also very much appreciated by the Southeast Asian countries. China was invited to take part in meetings of the Association of Southeast Asian Nations (ASEAN) as an observer. China also began to extend development aid to some countries in the region, a foreshadowing of the Belt and Road Initiative, which will be discussed later.

The border dispute with India was not resolved, but relations between the two states began to improve with a visit by Prime Minister Rajiv Gandhi in 1988, and warmed further through the 1990s. China also entered into agreements with South Korea, which had become a major trade partner and the source of the largest percentage of foreign students coming to study in China. The PRC and the Republic of Korea established formal diplomatic relations in 1992, while being careful to maintain its long-established close links with the DPRK. China played an important role in convening the Six-Party Talks with the US, Japan, Russia, and the two states on the peninsula, aimed at resolving issues around the nuclear program of the DPRK. These talks broke down under the George W. Bush administration, which returned to a posture of relentless hostility towards Pyongyang, but China had demonstrated its continuing support for the security of North Korea.

Central Asia became a very important arena for China after the breakup of the Soviet Union in 1991. In 1996, a Treaty of Enhancing Military Mutual Trust in the Border Areas was signed by China, Russia, Kazakhstan, Tajikistan, and Kyrgyzstan in Shanghai. Annual meetings began the next year, and in 2001, Uzbekistan joined this grouping, which then became known as the Shanghai Cooperation Organization (SCO). Only Turkmenistan of the former Soviet republics in the region declined to take part. In the following years Mongolia, Iran, India, and Pakistan were given observer status. The SCO is one of the largest regional organizations in the world, covering some two-thirds of the area of Eurasia and encompassing half the population of the world. In 1997, China also reached an agreement with Kazakhstan to develop a pipeline for oil to run from the Caspian Sea area to Xinjiang. Economic and security relations in Central Asia have remained a priority for China to the present day.

The year 2008 became critical in China's relations with the West, and indeed the rest of the world. China hosted the Olympic Games and put on a tremendous opening ceremony which impressed the world with China's accomplishments and capabilities. Hosting the Olympics was a clear demonstration of China's reemergence as an important participant in global affairs. Billions of people around the world saw China on their televisions as a modern, moderately prosperous society, a country totally transformed from the poverty and humiliation of the century when Western imperialism had dominated and exploited it. Leaders from around the world attended the games, a further recognition of the legitimacy and prestige of the People's Republic.

Even as the Olympic Games were taking place, however, the economies of the United States and its capitalist junior partner states were going into financial freefall. The United States' position at the heart of the global capitalist system meant that as it saw several of its major financial institutions collapse and a massive crisis in its housing market unfold, the effects of this spread rapidly to Britain, Germany, and other European countries, and even to some places in Asia, Africa, and Latin America which were enmeshed with loans and other financial shenanigans. Millions of ordinary people lost their homes and jobs, and hundreds of billions of taxpayer funds were given to banks and investment firms to ensure their continued profitability. It was crystal clear that in capitalist countries it is the interests of the wealthy that come first, rather than the needs of working people.

The financial crisis that broke out in 2008 impacted China as well. The People's Republic was not caught up in the shady financial schemes of derivatives and subprime mortgages, but it was vulnerable to the sharp decline in Western consumer demand as people scrambled to cope with the devastation of their lives. China had been a major supplier of consumer goods to US retailers like Walmart, but when so many people suddenly had no money to spend, orders for goods from China evaporated. This resulted in some twenty million workers in China being laid off. Fortunately, unlike in the capitalist economies where people who lost their jobs were basically cast out on the streets to fend for themselves, all citizens of China have a household registration, a core feature of the socialist system which entitles them to basic social services such as housing, health care, and educational opportunities for their children. The workers laid off from the great factories in Shenzhen, Zhuhai, and other areas, mostly on the southern coast, could return to the home villages where their household registrations would have been in place. This does not mean that they were living lives of luxury. The provision of social services, especially in rural China, was truly basic, but it was more than sufficient to sustain people at a decent level of material security. Meanwhile, the government and party were working to reorient China's economy to reduce its dependence of exports. China would remain a major exporter, but more resources were to be directed towards enhancing domestic consumer demand, in order to revive production for home markets. These policies, along with continuing overall growth of the economy, allowed the laid off workers to either return to their former jobs or to seek new employment opportunities, so that within a year or so the vast majority were once more at work. Indeed, though China's annual GDP growth dropped from a peak of 14.2 percent in 2007, it remained at a robust 9.7 percent in 2008, and rose to 10.2 percent in 2009. As it had during the Asian financial crisis of 1997, China weathered the 2008 crisis better than any of the Western capitalist economies, many of which, including the United States, continue to feel the effects of that meltdown today.

China's ability to navigate the 2008 financial crisis and its commitment to providing support for its laid-off workers through its socialist infrastructure did not go unnoticed in the West. The Obama administration's foreign policy team was already considering shifts in its priorities. The "War on Terror" was becoming less of an obsession as the situation in Iraq had descended into dysfunctional chaos and the fighting in Afghanistan appeared to have settled into a kind of stasis with US occupation forces propping up a corrupt and ineffective government, but with the Taliban seemingly no longer a serious threat. Even as fighting intensified in Syria, some US policymakers were reappraising the relationship with China. The dreams of regime change there, which had underpinned US thinking for more than two decades, had not come to fruition, and the demonstration of the resilience of the socialist system in the 2008 crisis was a further cause for reflection on the prospects for subordinating China to the global capitalist order.

In China as well, there was a developing sense that the project of reform and opening had yielded sufficient results, that the productive economy had grown, and that social wealth had been accumulated to a point where it was possible to begin to address the contradictions which had emerged over the previous decades. A new sense of pride in what had been achieved and a new confidence in their capacity for further success was spreading. The twin accomplishments of putting on the Olympics and managing the financial crisis were making it clear that the era of accommodation with global capitalism and imperialism might be coming to an end. China still wanted to remain engaged with the rest of the world, but it felt like the time was coming for adopting a new posture, a more proactive and generative attitude. The reappraisals of the US-China relationship taking place in both Washington and Beijing at the end of the first decade of the twenty-first century would result in dramatic shifts on the part of both countries. Those changes, and the new realities which have emerged from them, will be the focus of the third part of this book.

PART THREE

CHAPTER 6: 2011-2020

As the second decade of the twenty-first century got underway, profound changes were taking place in China's relations with the West and the rest of the world. The years 2011 and 2012 would prove to be, quite literally, a pivotal moment in global affairs. US political elites had long nurtured a dream of regime change in China, a faith that China's economic reforms would somehow inevitably lead to the overthrow of the socialist system and the emergence of a new government in Beijing. This in turn would totally unleash the forces of capital in the country and bring China into its proper place as a compliant cog in the machinery of global capitalism—but that dream had proven to be illusory. It was increasingly clear that China, under the leadership of the Communist Party, was not going to abandon the goals of the revolution: to improve the lives of the people and to build a society of prosperity in which the social distribution of the value produced by labor would be the new socialist normal. The Obama administration, which presented itself as a progressive, peace-loving force for change, undertook to reshape US foreign policy through new campaigns of aggression around the world, centered around a new posture of hostility towards China.

And in China, too, a new sense of self-confidence, as well as a recognition that the success of the reform policies and the accomplishments of the previous decades, had brought the country to the threshold of what they called a "moderately prosperous society." The remarkable growth of the economy had raised material standards of living for over a billion Chinese people and had given China sufficient resources to begin to address the contradictions of development which had arisen in the course of reform. New leadership took the helm, and China would no longer adopt a posture of accommodation towards US and global capitalism. The People's Republic was about to set out on new paths in its relations with the West, and with the developing countries of Asia, Africa, and Latin America.

The United States launched its new aggressive policy towards China in two salvoes late in 2011. President Obama, during visits to Australia and Indonesia, made a series of statements setting out his plan for a "Pivot to Asia." This was to be a major reallocation of US military assets, largely to East and Southeast Asia. Obama felt that the US had essentially prevailed in the "War on Terror," and that China, which had undergone rapid growth of its economy and demonstrated the resilience of its socialist system during the 2008 global financial crisis, should now be the main concern of US policy. China's rise and its reemergence as a major economic center and significant participant in world affairs was seen as a threat to US global hegemony. US corporate and political elites had enjoyed great power and privilege over many decades since the end of World War II, and especially since the end of the Cold War, and they were loath to see anything erode their domination of other countries. Although China had been a source of great profits for US capital since the 1980s, its refusal to succumb to regime change and its persistence in pursuit of a socialist future could no longer be tolerated. China needed to be contained and, if possible, derailed from its path of progress and development.

In tandem with Obama's announcement of the "Pivot to Asia," Secretary of State Hillary Clinton published an article in the journal *Foreign Policy* calling for a new "American Pacific Century." From the late 1800s to the second half of the twentieth century, the United States had pursued a policy of imperialist expansionism in the Pacific and East Asia, first acquiring small islands as naval stations, then overthrowing the independent monarchy of Hawai'i in 1895, and then seizing the Philippines from Spain and brutally repressing the independence movement there in a war from 1898–1907. Throughout these years, US American drug dealers, backed by their supporters in Congress and with the US Navy and Marines providing security for their operations, had played a major role in the opium trade in China. As Japan modernized and competed with the US for dominance in the western Pacific, it became inevitable that a clash between these powers would take place, eventually resulting in the war of 1937–1945 and concluding with the barbaric atomic bombing of the civilian populations of Hiroshima and Nagasaki in August 1945. Clinton now saw China's success in development as undermining the United States' power to continue to dominate the region, and she issued her call for a new round of US imperialist expansion.

One year after the United States' "Pivot to Asia," on November 15, 2012, Xi Jinping was elected General Secretary of the Communist Party of China at the Eighteenth Party Congress. He was also named as chair of the Central Military Commission. Li Keqiang became Prime Minister at this time as well. In March 2013, Xi was also elected President of the People's Republic. The election of these two leaders set the stage for a new era in China, in which a new attitude would become manifest both on the domestic scene and in China's relations with other countries. The age of accommodation with global capitalism and US imperialism was coming to an end. While this had been a necessary phase of the reform project, the effects of maintaining a low profile for socialism, while never abdicating the leading role of the CPC in guiding the reform process, had spilled over into a low-intensity political culture, both within the party and in society at large. The Chinese scholar Wang Hui refers to this as a kind of "depoliticized politics," in which most people simply seek to get along, to pursue their private interests, and are content with a government which creates conditions of stability that enable their pursuits. This kind of attitude had become widespread and had even affected many members of the CPC. Now there was to be a recommitment to, as Xi Jinping put it, fulfilling the original mission of the revolution—to improve the lives of the Chinese people and to build a socialist future for the country. There was a renewed emphasis on Marxism in study by party units and members, most strongly signaled by a meeting of the Political Bureau of the CPC at which *The Communist Manifesto* was read and discussed. Party units within economic, social, and governmental entities were reinvigorated. On a broader front, the party promoted a vision of the "China dream" in which socialist values of cooperation, collaboration, and compassion were emphasized. This renewed emphasis on Marxist theory, as well as the need to apply it creatively to the existing realities of China, was a kind of rectification program to ensure that the party would continue to play its leading role in development. In doing so, there was a lively and serious dedication to the socialist work of developing socialism with Chinese characteristics.

This renewed and enhanced level of political engagement was critical for the party to be able to grapple with the contradictions of development, from corruption and inequality to the existential crisis of environmental stresses and global warming. A massive anti-corruption campaign was launched, aimed at ferreting out government and party officials who were abusing their power and serving their private interests rather than devoting themselves to the needs of the people. This campaign, which continues to the present day, had brought cadres at every level of the system to justice, from local villages to the Political Bureau and the top ranks of the People's Liberation Army. It cannot be said that corruption has been totally eliminated, but the extent and intensity of this problem has been greatly reduced, and those in positions of authority who are tempted to succumb to corrupt behavior know that they are likely to be found out and prosecuted.

China also undertook a long-term project to raise those people in the country who were still below the definition of absolute poverty, the equivalent of $1.10 a day, above that line of demarcation. This would take years to accomplish and involved not only the allocation of material resources from the fund of social accumulation which had been built up over previous decades, but also the mobilization of large numbers of volunteers to go to many of the remote areas where pockets of poverty remained. The spirit of socialist solidarity demonstrated in the anti-poverty campaign was yet another sign of the vitality of China's political project. China achieved this goal in 2022 and remains committed to further enhancing the lives of all of its people.

The challenges of environmental degradation, both within the country and on a global scale, were becoming more evident every year. The process of industrial development, which lay at the heart of China's economic transformation, had generated serious pollution and other stresses on the ecosystem. As China entered the "new era," it was finally possible to begin to address these concerns as well. The government was able to direct investment towards key areas, including the development of alternative energy production and infrastructure designed to reduce the country's carbon footprint. This is of course a long-term project, but once again it demonstrates the capacity of the socialist system of planning to focus on specific problems and devote the resources of social accumulation to their resolution. Over the following years, China emerged as the world leader in both research and development of alternative energy, including wind, hydro, and solar power, and in the actual deployment and utilization of these technologies. The work of coping with the existential challenge of climate change and global warming continues in China and must be further deepened as the rest of the world lags behind.

The early years of the Xi Jinping–Li Keqiang administration were largely devoted to getting these and other domestic initiatives underway. But the transformation of China's relations with other countries was also starting, though this did not happen overnight. There were major developments in global affairs to which China's response was initially one of alignment with, or at least not overt opposition to, the United States' imperialist agenda. In 2011, as the "Pivot to Asia" was already being planned at the State Department and in the White House, popular movements against the corrupt and anti-democratic governments in North Africa broke out. Starting in Tunisia and then spreading to Egypt and other countries, mass movements arose calling for political change. The United States paid lip service to the democratic aspirations of people across the region, but did not wish to see the actual empowerment of ordinary working people. The Mubarak government was overthrown in Egypt, but the hopes of the people for a new order were frustrated as a military regime backed by the United States finally took power and suppressed the popular movement.

The United States seized upon unrest in Libya as a pretext for overthrowing the government of Muammar Gaddafi, who had been an outspoken critic of US imperialism. The oil riches of Libya were also of great interest to US corporate elites. The United States and their allies in Britain and France put forward United Nations Resolution 1783 to obtain authorization for NATO to launch an air war against Libya in March 2011. This campaign of bombing was approved by the Security Council. China and Russia both abstained from the vote. Both countries are permanent members of the Security Council with veto power, but they chose not to exercise this. For China especially, this reflected the lingering posture of accommodation with the West that had been in place since the 1980s. The United States also turned its military power loose on Syria, where there was a movement in opposition to the Ba'athist government of Bashar al-Assad. The US got another resolution through the United Nations Security Council for their actions in Syria, and once again China and Russia abstained. We can see that the policy of accommodation with the United States was still in place on the eve of the "new era." US military interventions were also underway in other parts of Africa, including Mali and Somalia. Even as Obama was preparing to declare the "Pivot to Asia," US interventionism on other parts of the world was actually on the rise. China, although refraining from vetoing the US-backed resolutions in the Security Council, took serious notice of this.

In 2013, the United States urged the Philippines, its former colony where it maintains military interests, to file a claim against China with the Permanent Court of Arbitration (PCA) in The Hague, the Netherlands, challenging China's assertion of sovereignty over areas of the South China Sea within what is known as the "Nine Dash Line." The PCA is an independent body that is not part of the United Nations, even though the claim made by the Philippines was supposedly based on a UN convention. The United States exempts itself from the jurisdiction of this body as well as from the International Court of Justice unless it specifically chooses to allow the court to consider a case against it. The Philippines action in filing this claim was basically a propaganda move by the US. China pointed out that agreements signed with the Philippines obligated the Manila government to resolve disputes between the two states through bilateral negotiations and declined to take part in the arbitration case.

Not surprisingly, the PCA ruled in favor of the Philippines. The ruling has no binding affect, but it has become a standard trope in US propaganda against China. One thing to note is that the central issue in the dispute, the "Nine Dash Line," is not a claim that has been made up by the People's Republic. The previous government, the Republic of China, led by the Guomindang nationalists, maintained the same claim, as do the local authorities on Taiwan. The Philippines did not include the Taiwan claim in their case, further demonstrating the real goal of their actions, which was to demonize China. US politicians and media pundits, who claim to support Taiwan, all ignore the fact that the Nationalists themselves were the first to assert the "Nine Dash Line" based on the territorial extent of the last imperial dynasty, the Qing, from which the authority of the Republic descended.

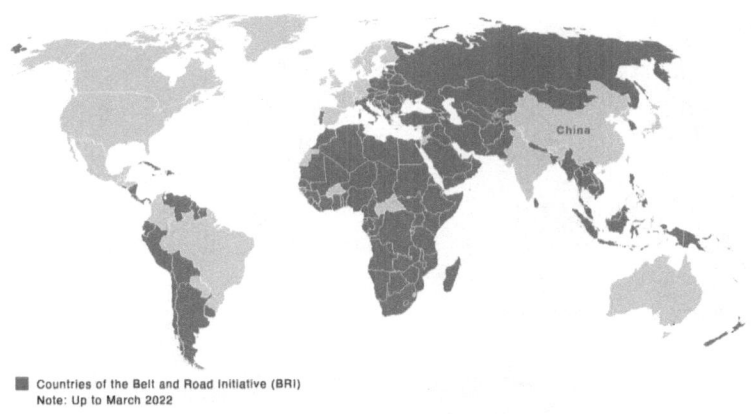

Participants in the Belt and Road Initiative. Map: Tina Duong

China's position in the South China Sea remains a point of serious contention between China and the US, and will be discussed further in the last chapter.

China's strong stance over the Philippines' claim was an initial indicator that the era of accommodation with the United States was over. The Obama administration was busy redeploying military forces to the Indian and Pacific Oceans to encircle China and adopting a rhetoric of confrontation and containment. Xi Jinping's government did not bow down to the United States' will, but rejected the Philippine's actions and repudiated the PCA's ruling. At the same time, China was engaging in bilateral discussions with other states in Southeast Asia which also had their own claims to some portions of the South China Sea, such as Vietnam or Indonesia. China was working on joint development projects with ASEAN member states. They were becoming more proactive, pursuing their own interests. The year 2013 also saw the launch of the One Belt, One Road Initiative.

The One Belt, One Road Initiative, which has come to be referred to more commonly as just the Belt and Road Initiative (BRI), was inaugurated in September 2013 during a visit to Kazakhstan by Xi Jinping. It was initially referred to as the "Silk Road Economic Belt," hearkening back to the overland trade routes which had linked imperial China to Central Asia, India, Persia, and Europe for more than two millennia. Soon, as other aspects of the program began to come into place

Overland rail routes connecting China with Europe. Map: Tina Duong

and the scale of the endeavor greatly expanded, it came to be known as the Belt and Road Initiative, and this is how it is referred to today.

The BRI is a massive program of aid and investment, aimed at developing infrastructure for trade among developing countries, mostly in Asia, Africa, and Latin America, but including a few European states as well. As we will see, it is part of an even larger project to create a whole new system of international exchange and cooperation. In its early years, much of the focus was on developing overland routes across Eurasia to facilitate and expand the delivery of goods produced in China to markets in Europe and beyond. This especially involved building or updating rail lines through Kazakhstan and other Central Asian lands to connect with existing systems in Russia and the rest of Europe. As these came online, it became possible to ship goods from Shanghai or the SEZs in southern China to destinations like Rotterdam in Europe much faster than it would be to send them by ship. In conjunction with the pipeline projects mentioned in the last chapter, the BRI created stronger linkages between China and the Central Asian states as investment in local economic developments grew along the new trade routes.

This first phase of overland development soon expanded to include projects in cities and countries around the Indian Ocean and in Africa, creating a new Maritime Silk Road, echoing the complex interactions of seafaring traders dating back to Roman times. As noted earlier, China was already involved in railway projects and other development work in Africa as early as the 1960s. With the BRI, the level of China's engagement rose significantly. The need for aid and investment in Africa had greatly intensified after the collapse of the Soviet Union in 1991. During the Cold War, the United States sent aid to various African countries in the hope of blocking Soviet influence and undermining local anti-imperialist and socialist movements. But once the rivalry with the Soviets ended, the United States lost interest in Africa and radically reduced its assistance to the continent. As China reached a level of development and moderate prosperity that allowed it to devote resources to new projects, Africa became a major focus of BRI activities. The construction or renovation of port facilities in many parts of Africa was an important first step, opening up access to markets within host countries and enabling easier entry into global networks for exports.

One point must be clear: the BRI was not a charitable undertaking. It was not a giveaway program, a philanthropic exercise. Western bourgeois critics of China often argue that China seeks to profit from the access it gains to overseas markets. This is certainly true, but it is no reason the criticize the BRI. China is quite clear that the objective of the program is to develop and enhance trade relations among the participating countries. This is a process of mutual benefit. The host country gains infrastructure, investments, and other ancillary benefits. China often includes the construction of facilities which are not of immediate economic benefit, like schools, hospitals, or sports arenas. But China also wants to grow its trade with the countries where it is investing. The BRI is good for both the recipients of Chinese support and for China itself. This not a matter of neocolonialism. China does not attach political conditions to its aid, nor does it interfere in the internal affairs of the member countries, unlike the US-backed International Monetary Fund or the World Bank, whose austerity programs have caused massive suffering for working people from Argentina to Zimbabwe.

Much of the funding of BRI activities is in the form of loans by China to the host country. These are offered at interest rates below international market levels. China has been very flexible in rescheduling loan repayments in instances where a particular project or country has been unable to maintain the original agreement. There have been instances when a recipient country has encountered serious difficulties in its own finances and budgeting, and in a handful of cases this has resulted in assets which had been constructed with Chinese funds being transferred to Chinese ownership in order to keep them functioning. The port facilities built for Sri Lanka are one example of this, which has been seized on by Western bourgeois media and politicians to accuse China of creating a "debt trap" to exploit poor developing nations. But this is far from the case. The overwhelming reality is that countries who join the BRI see their economies grow and are able, with the enhanced revenues thus generated, to repay the low-interest loans which made that growth possible. China is not establishing colonial rule or domination over the BRI member states. It continues to honor the Five Principles of Peaceful Coexistence which have been the foundation of the country's foreign policy since the 1950s, including mutual benefit, respect for the sovereignty of all countries, and noninterference in the internal affairs of other countries.

The BRI was only one component of a broader effort to develop a new global order of trade and exchange among countries not wishing to remain under the domination of the United States. Through its control of the settlement of international payments, almost all of which had been denominated in US dollars since the end of World War II, and through the instruments of the International Monetary Fund and the World Bank, the United States has presided over a network of economic mechanisms that gave them incredible power to manipulate the affairs of nations, large and small, all around the world. While the Soviet Union and the socialist states of Eastern Europe had provided an alternative for some countries, with the end of that era in 1989–1991, US global hegemony had become almost universal. As the "new era" in China got going in the 2010s, a number of policies and programs were launched to create alternative mechanisms for international economic relations. The BRI formed a kind of core for this, but was by no means the full extent of the project.

Late in 2013, Xi Jinping proposed the creation of the Asian Infrastructure Investment Bank (AIIB) as an alternative to the IMF and the World Bank. The AIIB rapidly became a reality, with more than one hundred countries becoming participating members. The AIIB was meant to provide loans for countries seeking to build new infrastructure and was specifically aimed at promoting investment in green technologies and in cyber connectivity, seeking to address both concerns about climate change and to bring developing countries to higher levels of technological capability. The United States tried to discourage countries from joining the AIIB, but even some of its close allies such as South Korea and Great Britain chose to join anyway. Since its inception, the AAIB has grown significantly and has played an ever-increasing role in financing developments projects, not only in Asia but in Africa and Latin America as well.

The AIIP provided a new source of funding for development projects, but international settlements, the payment of transactions taking place between entities in different countries, were still almost entirely conducted in US dollars through a system known as the Society for Worldwide Interbank Financial Telecommunications (SWIFT). By controlling the flow of payments across borders, the United States held incredible leverage over countries around the world. It was able to develop and maintain its regime of sanctions, its weapon of choice in the manipulation and domination of states to ensure their obedience to—or punish their disobedience from—US wishes. History has shown that these sanctions rarely achieve their supposed intended effects: to force political leaders in targeted countries to change their policies and actions and bring them in line with US dictates. Rather, they have the effect of inflicting suffering on the masses of ordinary people. This is a brutal, blunt instrument of US imperial power, which has been deployed around the world, from Cuba and North Korea to Iran and Myanmar, and many other lands. China now sought a way to reduce the United States' power and weaponization of the SWIFT system of international settlements. Instead, it looked to create new institutions and relationships which would allow countries to opt for alternative mechanisms for the payments of their obligations.

In 2015, China began to develop the Cross-Border Interbank Payment System (CIPS). This new network would enable international payments to be made using the *renminbi*, also known as the *yuan*, the Chinese currency. This did not immediately lead to everyone converting from SWIFT to CIPS. The dominant place of the US-backed system remains, but China has provided settlement capabilities to well over one hundred countries in Asia, Africa, Latin America, and Europe, and the project continues to be advanced. China is not alone in seeking to promote alternatives to the SWIFT system. Russia created its own *ruble*-denominated settlement system in 2014. Malaysia has promoted the idea of creating a new system of international payments based not on replacing the US dollar with another single currency, but with a mechanism using a basket of currencies. China has supported and encouraged these and other efforts to free countries from dependence on international financial and economic institutions controlled or dominated by the United States.

Another important development in China's international activities was the formation of a group of nations with shared interests in economic development and in moving towards a more multicentric world order. This group, which first came together in 2009, originally included Brazil, Russia, India, and China, with South Africa joining one year later. Known as BRICS, the organization added new members in January 2024, including Iran, Egypt, Ethiopia, and the United Arab Emirates. Saudi Arabia is not a member but takes part in some BRICS activities as an invited observer. BRICS holds annual summit meetings and works together on cooperative projects of development and investment. The New Development Bank was created in 2014 as another funding source for development projects in the member states and for nonmember states which chose to apply. The BRICS countries cover about 30 percent of the world's land surface and account for 45 percent of the global population. Together their economies contribute about 33 percent of global economic production. BRICS is an organization within which China plays an important role, but it is not a creation of China's nor does China seek to dominate it. BRICS is a multilateral intergovernmental group, and was conceived as a counterweight to the G7, the cluster of capitalist nations led by the United States that seeks to dominate global economic affairs. BRICS brought together the biggest countries outside of the capitalist core with the greatest economic clout in order to push back against Western imperialist domination and to reshape the global economic order in a more equitable, multicentric way.

In 2016, US political elites were shocked by the election of Donald Trump as president of the United States. Although himself a wealthy member of the bourgeoisie, Trump was a loose cannon, a rogue figure operating beyond the usual parameters of US ruling-class politics. His primary objective was to enrich himself and his cronies, and to use the government as a means to punish his various enemies and opponents. Trump enunciated a foreign policy of "America first" and often ignored long-established policies and positions. While presenting himself as an "outsider" who appealed to a voter base of alienated working-class people, Trump, of course, was actually just another rich man who wanted to get richer, not caring who was exploited or dispossessed in the process.

Trump's foreign policies, if they can be called that, were as erratic as the rest of his activities. He initially seemed to seek a resolution of tensions with the Democratic People's Republic of Korea, meeting with the North Korean leader Kim Jong Un in Singapore in 2018 and in Hanoi in 2019. But this initiative, which was strongly opposed by the foreign policy establishment and most mainstream politicians and pundits, fell apart, and Trump then resumed the usual US imperialist posture of hostility towards the DPRK. Trump also began with an apparently friendly relationship with Russian leader Vladimir Putin, but that, too, went through subsequent transformation into an attitude of estrangement. Trump berated US vassal states in Europe for not paying enough for NATO protection.

For US elites, China was the biggest concern. As China became more assertive in world affairs and was clearly no longer willing to subordinate itself to Western interests, the Democratic administration of Barack Obama had launched the "Pivot to Asia" to contain and constrain China, hoping to slow or derail it progress and development. Trump now sought to outdo Obama in his anti-China rhetoric and actions. Even before being sworn in as president, Trump signaled his aggressive approach to China by making a phone call to Tsai Ying-wen, the president of the local government on Taiwan. No US president or president-elect had had direct contact with a high Taiwan official since 1979 when formal diplomatic relations were finalized with the PRC. When asked about whether his administration would adhere to the One China policy, Trump suggested that continuing to recognize that there is only one China might be dependent on the Beijing government agreeing to US terms on issues of trade.

Once he assumed office, Trump set about dismantling much of the policy package of US relations with China. He broke off bilateral negotiations for a trade agreement, terminated the Joint Commission on Commerce and Trade, and shut down the Strategic and Economic Dialogue meetings. Perhaps the most important action of the Trump administration was the declaration of a trade war with China through the imposition of tariffs. These tariffs often charged 25 percent on a wide range of goods imported from the country. This trade war with China was part of an overall attempt to reduce the United States' trade deficit with China and many other countries, and to promote the purchase of domestic products by US consumers. This plan was largely designed for domestic political consumption: these policies led to higher prices for ordinary people, but did not result in a decline in imports nor in a revival of manufacturing in the US. China retaliated by placing tariffs on some US products, but these accounted for only a tiny fraction of trade between the countries, and were more of a political gesture than an actual attempt to limit imports.

On December 1, 2018, the vice-chair and chief financial officer of Huawei, a major Chinese tech company, was arrested in Canada on orders from the United States. Meng Wanzhou was accused of having facilitated technology transfers to Iran in violation of US sanctions. Huawei is one of China's most successful, innovative high-tech enterprises, and has been a target of US corporate and political powers for many years. This was yet another example of the United States arrogating to itself the right to intervene in the internal affairs of any country, anywhere in the world, without regard to sovereignty or interests. Meng was held under house arrest until September 2021, when she was finally released and returned immediately to China. The judicial kidnapping and detention of Meng was a crude attempt to intimidate her and other Chinese business leaders. It was an integral part of the emerging campaign to thwart China's development of consumer-product technologies, especially computer chips and products made with them. This campaign would evolve in the coming years to be perhaps the most significant component of US efforts to derail economic and technological advancement in the People's Republic.

The year 2020 was to be an important year in China's relations with the West and other parts of the world. The emergence of the COVID-19 virus and the effects of the ensuing pandemic will be addressed in the next chapter. The Trump administration deepened its hostility towards China and pushed its agenda on multiple fronts. The demonization of China as an abuser of human rights was taken to new levels and linked to economic objectives. The cooperation between China and the United States in combating terrorism by

Islamic fundamentalist groups, including those operating in Xinjiang, had come to a halt before this, and the State Department no longer included Uighur terror groups in its list of such entities. In June 2020, Congress passed an act authorizing sanctions against China for nonexistent concentration camps. United States mass media was filled with reports of abuses in Xinjiang, most of which emanated from a single source, a radical Christian visionary who was told by "God" that Uighurs were being persecuted. This source, Adrian Zenz, who works for the rabidly anti-China "Victims of Communism Memorial Foundation" funded by the US government, was routinely quoted as an expert on Xinjiang, despite his not having been in China for more than a decade and the fact that he does not speak Uighur. In July 2020, the US banned trade with Chinese companies which were accused of abuses in Xinjiang.

The Trump years also saw repeated statements by government officials characterizing China as the greatest threat to the United States, and portraying Chinese students and scholars in the US as potential agents of hostile intelligence organizations. Under Trump, the so-called China Initiative was launched by the Department of Justice, targeting researchers from China and accusing them of spying. High-profile arrests were made of Chinese scholars, and sometimes their US American colleagues, generating scare headlines in the media. No one was ever convicted of espionage or any related offense, but when the charges were dropped, media coverage was minimal at best. The purpose of these arrests was not to seek the truth or protect the US, but was to frighten the people of the United States and intimidate Chinese people living in or visiting the US. The China Initiative was renamed later as a cosmetic attempt to mask anti-China activities.

The years 2019 and 2020 were also the years in which the Confucius Institute program was eliminated by the US government. The Confucius Institutes had been educational programs at US universities in partnership with Chinese academic institutions, primarily designed to provide Chinese language educational services. Teachers from China came to the US to work as teachers at universities and secondary schools to offer language instruction in modern Chinese. These Confucius Institutes often also offered cultural programming, including speakers' series, lunar new year celebrations, and films or other cultural performances. Founded in the early 2000s, by 2019 there were almost one hundred Confucius Institutes in the United States. Anti-China elements in some places regularly accused the Confucius Institutes of being tools of the CPC that promoted communist "propaganda." As with the China Initiative, these charges were baseless, but the accusations got lots of press coverage and served to further demonize China.

The State Department and the Department of Defense (DoD) undertook various efforts to undermine and eliminate the Confucius Institute program. Ever greater restrictions were put on the visas of Chinese teachers coming to US universities. Beginning in 2019, the Defense Department told universities that were hosting Confucius Institutes that if they wanted to continue to receive DoD grant funding for research, which regularly amounted to tens of millions of dollars, they would have to shut down their Confucius Institutes. All but a tiny handful did so. The campaign against the Confucius Institutes was part of the overall bipartisan hostility towards China, but it was also specifically driven by the need to keep US Americans from having any direct knowledge of China and its social and political realities. The demonization of China was largely dependent upon the fact that most US Americans had no information about China other than what the politicians and the corporate media told them. Those who actually visited or worked there quickly saw that China was nothing like the authoritarian dystopia hyped by US media, entertainment, and politicians. Eliminating the Confucius Institutes closed what had been an important window for the free flow of knowledge and information across the Pacific. Other government-sponsored cultural exchange programs which had operated for years were also shut down by the end of 2020.

Perhaps the most reckless and dangerous dimension of US aggressiveness towards China has been over national sovereignty. Ever since Nixon's visit to Beijing and Shanghai in 1972, the United States government has officially adhered to the One China policy, as first expressed in the Shanghai Communique and reiterated in several subsequent agreements. It is the public position of the US government that there is only one China, the People's Republic, and that Taiwan is part of the country. Yet throughout the seventy-five years of the PRC's history, the US has funded and armed the local authorities on the island, and since the "Pivot to Asia" it has actively promoted political forces calling for Taiwan to be an independent state. The Trump administration continued these illegal actions, with US navy vessels routinely transiting Chinese territorial waters between the mainland and island, and concluding with a $1.8 billion weapons deal in October 2020. China regularly stated its opposition to US arms sales and other acts of interference in China's internal affairs. The position of the government in Beijing has been and remains that the question of the status Taiwan is one that comes down from history and which needs to be resolved by the Chinese people on both sides of the strait in their own way and in their own time, without the interference of outside parties. While maintaining this principle, China has acted with great restraint in response to US provocations.

National sovereignty is also the issue in the South China Sea. This is an area over which China asserts its historical control. As noted above, the modern legal claim to areas of the South China Sea and the delineation of that claim with the "Nine Dash Line" originated with the Nationalist government in the 1940s based on China's long historical presence in the maritime region. The People's Republic inherited this territory as it did the rest of the country when it came to power in 1949. Several other countries in Southeast Asia also have claims over some specific parts of the South China Sea, and China has engaged in bilateral negotiations with them with the goal of a resolution to conflicting positions. The United States, which backs the local government on Taiwan that makes exactly the same territorial assertions, rejects China's sovereignty over the area and routinely carries out provocative naval exercises in the waters of the South China Sea, often passing within a few miles of islands that are clearly Chinese territory. While the United States claims a two-hundred-mile "exclusion zone" off US coasts, it only recognizes a twelve-mile limit to other countries waters. Under the false flag of "freedom of navigation," US ships have engaged in repeated acts of provocation, sometimes endangering Chinese vessels and their crews.

The year 2020, then, saw the relationship between China and the United States getting more and more fraught as the United States continued to escalate its aggressive actions aimed at thwarting China's development and blocking its reemergence as a significant participant in global affairs. This was a fool's errand—the transformation from a US-dominated unipolar world to one in which many countries were developing modern industrial economies and a more multi-centric geopolitical order, was and remains the basic dynamic of contemporary world history. It is a deep structural reconfiguration taking place in the world. China's role in this process is important, but not the totality of these changes. From 2011 to 2020, China had taken great steps to promote new institutions and infrastructure for this emerging era, from the BRI to the Asian Infrastructure Investment Bank, the Shanghai Cooperation Organization, and other international initiatives. China's success in growing its economy while retaining its socialist character was becoming a source of inspiration for people in places around the world.

But 2020 was also the year in which the COVID-19 pandemic erupted, which put tremendous stress on the lives of people in China and around the world. This would prove to be another test of China's socialist system and its relations with the wider world. As the 2020's advanced, there were both positive and negative aspects in global affairs, and these will be explored in the next, and final chapter.

CHAPTER 7: 2020-2024

The outbreak of the COVID-19 pandemic and the election of Cold War-leftover Joe Biden as president marked a transition to a more intense phase of US aggressions towards China which has continued to the present day. But the years 2020 to 2024 have also been a period during which China has become ever more effective and proactive in its international activities, carrying on the work of building a new infrastructure of trade and exchange systems free from the domination of US interests, and working for peace and justice for people in many crisis regions of the world, most notably in the Middle East and in the conflict in Ukraine. While US provocations have escalated in the South China Sea and the Taiwan Strait, China has displayed steady restraint while resolutely defending its sovereignty and territorial integrity. China's handling of the pandemic also once again demonstrated the resilience of its socialist system, as it saved millions of lives while accepting the costs in economic terms. China also became the world leader in providing vaccines to people around the planet, at little to no cost in poor and developing countries.

The virus which came to be known as COVID-19 was detected by medical personnel in Wuhan, in central China, at the very end of 2019 and beginning of 2020. China acted quickly to identify the genetic structure of the virus and shared that data with international health organizations immediately. As the seriousness of the situation became evident, China took prompt and effective measures to isolate and contain the spread of the virus, controlling the movement of people into and out of areas where infections were found. A massive

China constructed hospitals in a matter of weeks at the onset of the COVID-19 pandemic.
Photo: Zhong Min/Avalon

program of emergency hospital construction was launched, deploying socially accumulated resources to rapidly expand treatment capabilities. Research and development of vaccines was undertaken, and resulted in the creation and large-scale production of two vaccines which proved effective in treating and preventing infections. Saving lives and protecting the health of China's people were the top priorities for the party and the government, as well as for the millions of ordinary Chinese who volunteered to fight the pandemic—in hospitals and clinics, as deliverers of food and other supplies to people sheltering in their homes, and as providers of information and support to the public in a time of crisis and anxiety. Thanks to China's socialist system, over the almost three years that the Zero COVID policies were in place, fewer than six thousand people died of the virus.

In the United States, the Trump administration sought to further demonize China by spreading misinformation that the virus had been intentionally created in a lab, or that China had willfully spread the virus. The US capitalist system saw the pandemic as an opportunity to generate profits, and insurance companies, hospital corporations, and the pharmaceutical industry all made billions off the suffering of the country's citizens. Over 1.1 million people died as the US prioritized profits over human lives. Politicians and the mass media desperately sought to portray China's comprehensive program of COVID-19 suppression as some kind of totalitarian nightmare. Of course, in a land of 1.4 billion people there were of course instances in which problems occurred in implementing this massive undertaking, and the US media seized upon any report of people expressing frustration as a sign of the terrible repressiveness of the People's Republic. Meanwhile, hospitals across the United States were overrun by patients desperate for care, many of whom lost their lives because of cutbacks in public health provisions and the emphasis on profit-making in a society where most medical services are controlled by private corporations.

China's determination to save the lives of its people and the rapid development of vaccines also carried over into China's relations with other countries, especially those most in need of aid and assistance in coping with the pandemic. Overall, China delivered more than 1.6 billion doses of three different vaccines to countries around the world. The Asia-Pacific region, including India and Southeast Asia, received the greatest share, but Africa had more than 150 million doses delivered, almost all of which were donated free of charge; Latin America got almost 300 million, and even Europe received nearly 60 million. Where vaccines were not donated outright, they were sold at cost. China declared its vaccines to be a "global public good" rather than a commodity to be sold at a profit.

In the midst of the pandemic, as millions of ordinary people in the United States suffered the ravages of the virus, Joe Biden was elected president in November 2020. An unreconstructed Cold Warrior, Biden assumed office in January 2021 and immediately set out to deepen the United States' efforts to contain China's development and its growing role as a valuable member of the international community. Biden appointed anti-China hawks to lead his foreign policy team, including Secretary of State Anthony Blinken and National Security advisor Jake Sullivan. In March 2021, Blinken and Sullivan met with Wang Yi, China's foreign minister, and Yang Jiechi, a member of the Political Bureau of the CPC, in Anchorage, Alaska. Blinken and Sullivan launched an all-out attack on China, scolding Wang and Yang with finger-wagging gestures and condescending rhetoric. The Chinese diplomats responded forcefully, rejecting the United States' efforts to demonize and belittle China, clearly demonstrating the country's new posture of self-confidence and their refusal to bend to US intimidation. This encounter set the tone for the Biden administration's approach to China, which was to become more and more reckless and antagonistic over the coming years. Key areas of this intensification of hostility were the promotion of a narrative of China as pursuing repressive policies in Xinjiang, Tibet, and Hong Kong, the ramping up of tensions around the status of Taiwan, and the expansion of US Navy provocations in the South China Sea.

US politicians and the mass media have a long history of condemning China for violating the human rights of ethnic or religious minorities. As noted above, the CIA ran clandestine operations in Tibet for many years, using terrorist agents trained at a camp high in the mountains of Colorado. In order to both disrupt domestic society and to tarnish China's reputation internationally, propaganda presenting China as oppressing the Tibetans, and more recently the Muslim Uighurs of Xinjiang, goes hand in hand with covert efforts to promote separatist movements in those regions. The Biden administration has intensified these activities as part of its overall campaign to derail development and prosperity for the Chinese people. Biden and other politicians from both the bourgeois parties have adopted a rhetoric of "great power conflict" and invoked the trope of the "Thucydides trap" to legitimize their war mongering. The ancient Greek historian Thucydides argued that when an established "great power" is challenged by the rise of a new competitor, it is almost inevitable that they will eventually go to war. This is not actually sustained in the historical record, but it has been regularly deployed in order to argue for more and more military spending to prepare for a possible war with China. Demonizing China as a place where minority people face oppression helps to prepare people in the US to accept the need for war, and this tactic is designed to make people fear China and see it as an enemy. US politicians in the Biden era have even referred to China's policies in Xinjiang as "genocide," an absurd and entirely unsustainable charge made all the more ridiculous in light of both the United States' history of the eradication of indigenous societies within its expanding territories and its massive funding of Israel's war to destroy the Palestinian people.

While the vilification of China's supposed abuses in Tibet and Xinjiang—allegations which are not borne out by actual conditions in either region—is carried on through the media and in the halls of Congress, more serious threats to peace are being carried out in the

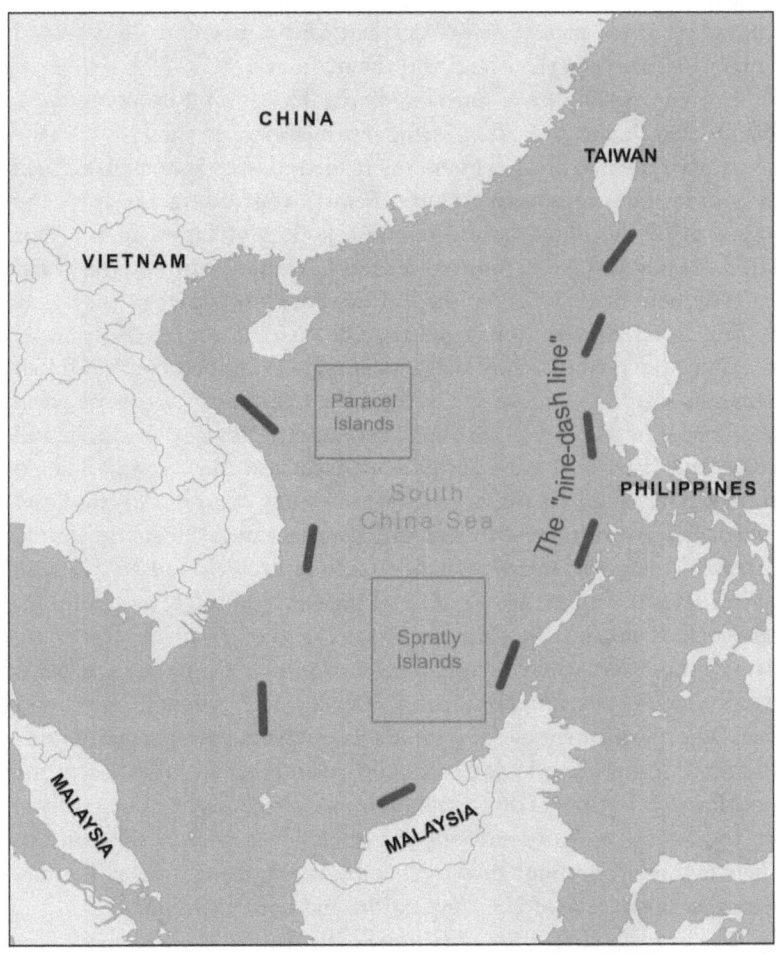

South China Sea. Map: Tina Duong

South China Sea and around the island of Taiwan. These are areas in which the United States asserts its exceptional right to maintain military operations and to violate the One China policy by supplying the local authorities on Taiwan with massive amounts of military material, even sending US military personnel to collaborate with local forces. The hypocrisy of the United States' conduct is stunning, as it claims to respect the long-established agreements signed by several administrations acknowledging the status of Taiwan as a part of

China, yet at the same time works relentlessly to promote division and separation between the island and the mainland.

In August 2022, the Speaker of the House of Representatives, Nancy Pelosi, and five other Democrat members of the House made a visit to Taiwan during which they made repeated statements aimed at promoting a separatist agenda. Pelosi's visit was made with the approval of the Biden administration, a clear violation of the One China policy. Other US political leaders have made stops on the island or have met with officials of the Taiwan government when they were in the United States. Ships from the US Pacific Fleet routinely travel through the Taiwan Strait along a course self-defined by the United States as international waters beyond the territory of any state, even though all of Taiwan is within two hundred miles of the mainland coast, the distance the US claims as an exclusion zone around its own shores. The US picks and chooses which rules it applies to itself and which it can use against others. All these actions reflect the United States' determination to challenge China's growth and its place in global affairs, even at the risk of sparking war. Indeed, several military leaders have taken to issuing predictions as to when such a war could break out, despite there being no indication that China has any plans to alter the status quo concerning Taiwan by force or in any other way. The government of the People's Republic has always maintained the position that Taiwan is part of China, and that the question of the political arrangements on the island is one which needs to be resolved by the people on both sides of the strait in their own time and in their own way, without interference from any third parties. China's restraint in the face of US provocations has been exemplary.

The situation in the South China Sea has been discussed above, but under the Biden administration, and with the enthusiastic support of both parties in Congress, the provocations being carried out by US naval forces have been made more frequent and more recklessly confrontational. Claiming to be protecting "freedom of navigation," which has never been challenged or impeded by China, US Navy vessels routinely challenge China's sovereignty and territorial integrity and sometimes directly confront PRC Coast Guard or PLA Navy ships in their normal performance of activities. Here, too, the real objective is to assert US hegemony, its self-proclaimed right to police the whole world and coerce other countries to comply with its will.

This is, again, all part of the agenda to contain China and inhibit its development and its participation in international activities.

Yet another dimension of the United States' efforts to demonize China has been its support, both overt and covert, for anti-government demonstrations, often morphing into violent riots, in Hong Kong. In 2019 and 2020, there had been major confrontations between anti-government groups and the Hong Kong police and local authorities. These were initially caused by the pending introduction of a law allowing for the government to extradite people charged with crimes back to Hong Kong. This law had originally been called for by local authorities on Taiwan in regard to a case of a Hong Kong man charged with sexual assault who had fled to Taiwan to escape prosecution. The protests rapidly developed, however, into attacks on government offices and officials, as well as on businesses or other establishments, some of which were firebombed or otherwise vandalized. These protests and riots were supported and encouraged by outside actors, including the US-funded National Endowment for Democracy, and were widely covered by Western mainstream media as a "pro-democracy" movement. News reports in the United States and other Western countries portrayed the rioters as progressive young people fighting the authoritarian Chinese state, and chose not to take notice of the violence, including firebombing a subway station as well as numerous assaults on police officers.

The spread of the COVID-19 pandemic contributed to the decline of these activities, and the Hong Kong government managed to restore normal order later in 2020, but US politicians have continued to forward their overall propaganda narrative, invoking the idea of Hong Kong as a place where China oppresses the people. Here, yet again, the reality is rather different, as Hong Kong has seen the slow but steady expansion of political participation under the Basic Law: it now has a multiparty electoral political system and its own distinctive local legal system that gives Hong Kong people rights and responsibilities never extended to them by the British colonialists in their century and a half of imperialist rule. The United States' efforts to subvert public order in Hong Kong as part of the broader campaign to weaken or roll back China's reemergence as a major economy and as a leading participant in world affairs founders on the realities of life in Hong Kong.

The United States has abandoned the fantasy of regime change in China and turned to a posture of outright antagonism, even contemplating and preparing for war with the People's Republic. Meanwhile, China has increasingly assumed a larger role in global affairs. While the United States can impose its will on its vassal states in much of Europe, South Korea, and Japan, more and more countries in Asia, Africa, and Latin America are coming to see China as both a source of aid and assistance in their efforts to develop their own economies. This aid comes without the conditions and controls imposed by Western lenders and governments, and offers a model of development aimed at improving the lives of its people rather for maximizing profits for a capitalist elite. China continues to pursue institutional innovations in international trade and finance aimed at giving countries alternatives to the established US-dominated global economic order, as discussed previously. The People's Republic has also engaged in a number of major diplomatic initiatives to promote peace and reduce tensions in various parts of the world, while the United States government, in thrall to the giant weapons manufacturing corporations of the military-industrial complex, pushes ahead with wars and military interventions around the world.

When the Cold War came to an end in the early 1990s, and the German Democratic Republic was absorbed into the German federal state, and the North Atlantic Treaty Organization (NATO), which had been formed early in the Cold War to confront the Soviet Union, saw opportunities to expand its power and project it to the east. However, in discussions with Russian leaders at the time, US Secretary of State James Baker promised Mikhail Gorbachev that NATO would not follow this course, and pledged that NATO would grow "not one inch to the east." Like many agreements and treaties made by the United States, this quickly proved to be a lie. Over the following years, NATO pursued eastern expansion, bringing former socialist states in Eastern Europe into the organization one after the other, despite repeated protests from Russia which viewed NATO's eastern thrust as a threat to its own security. This process culminated in February 2022, when Russia launched a special military operation in Ukraine both to protect ethnic Russian communities in the eastern part of the country and to push back against the threat of Ukraine being added to NATO, which would bring anti-Russian military forces right to its borders.

The situation in Ukraine became a dominant focus of US policy. The Biden administration sought to use the war there as a way to bleed the Russian economy and hopefully promote regime change in Russia. In this context, China took a strong stance in favor of a ceasefire in Ukraine and the resolution of the issues between the parties through negotiations. At the same time, China made it clear that it would maintain its close relationship with Russia, which had developed over the previous decade into one of major economic exchanges, and of a shared commitment to promoting a global geopolitical order not subordinated to US power. As noted above, China and Russia were already cooperating closely in the Shanghai Coordination Organization to promote stability and development in Central Asia. China and Russia have very different economic and social systems, but also common concerns and interests, which made their mutual support compelling. China has maintained its diplomatic and economic relationships with Ukraine as well, making repeated efforts to promote negotiations aimed at ending the fighting and resolving the underlying issues.

China has not been alone in rejecting the US narrative about the conflict in Ukraine. At the United Nations the General Assembly passed resolutions condemning Russia in 2022, 2023, and 2024, with 141 countries voting in favor. But the forty countries that either voted against the resolution or abstained, refusing to agree with the US-backed measure, represented half the world's population, including China, India, South Africa, Pakistan, and Vietnam. As more and more countries seek to get out from under US domination, the shifting nature of global relations is clearly reflected in these votes.

China's recent relations with other countries have not been merely reactive to US hostility, but have also been proactive, both in its efforts to build new institutional infrastructure and in diplomatic activity to address particular problems in critical areas. One very important arena of concern to China is the Middle East, and here China has been engaged in major efforts to resolve long-standing issues. The People's Republic has a long history of close relations with countries in the region, based on the Five Principles of Peaceful Coexistence that have guided its foreign policies since the 1950s. It has been a strong supporter of the rights of the Palestinian people to self-determination, but has also maintained diplomatic relations with

Israel. China's interests and activities in the Middle East follow the principles of respect for the sovereignty and territorial integrity of all countries, and noninterference in the internal affairs of other countries. In the last few years, China has made significant contributions to peace and stability among the Muslim states, many of which are participants in the Belt and Road Initiative.

After twenty years of war and occupation, the United States finally withdrew from Afghanistan in August 2021. This was quickly followed by the return of the Taliban to power and the proclamation of an Islamic Republic in the country. The US, which had presided over the death of many civilians and the collapse of much of Afghanistan's economy, followed its precipitous departure with the freezing of Afghan assets. This deprived the new Taliban government of resources desperately needed to address the massive humanitarian crisis the United States left in its wake. China shares a small border with Afghanistan but had taken an interest in the affairs of the country for many years. In the 2010s, the PRC had taken part in peacekeeping efforts there, and in 2015, had hosted meetings between the US-backed Afghan government and the Taliban, in Urumqi, Xinjiang. Discussions between the Chinese and the Taliban took place again in 2018. In the wake of the United States' retreat, China kept its embassy open and signaled its willingness to work with the new authorities. When the massive earthquake of June 2022 struck, China provided $7.5 million worth of relief assistance to the Taliban government and additional aid to the Afghan Red Crescent Society. China does not formally recognize the Taliban state, but it has continued to provide aid and assistance for the people of Afghanistan and promote peace between that country and its neighbors, including Pakistan and Iran.

In Pakistan itself, China has been working with the government to develop an economic corridor running from the border with Xinjiang Autonomous Region to the port of Gwadar on the Indian Ocean. This project was initiated in 2014 as part of the BRI and has become one of the largest projects of the initiative, incorporating rail and road building to facilitate the shipment of oil and natural gas, as well as the developing the energy-generating capacity in Pakistan and other spinoff benefits for the Pakistan economy. Since 2018, the focus in the energy sector has been on hydropower and other renewable sources, shifting away from the previous focus on coal-powered generation. Much of the financing for the China–Pakistan Economic Corridor has been the form of interest-free loans or outright grants. The project is still in various stages of construction and development, but has already had a large positive impact on Pakistan's economy. It has not been entirely without friction, however. Anti-government Islamic militants and fighters for a separatist movement in the south-western region of Baluchistan have attacked Chinese workers several times since 2017, with nearly twenty Chinese people killed. This has been a serious security concern, but both China and Pakistan remain committed to the completion of this massive program.

In March 2023, Wang Yi, China's foreign minister, announced the signing of an agreement between Saudi Arabia and the Islamic Republic of Iran. This was an historic event that dramatically reduced the tension between these states, with implications for political stability in other countries such as Syria, Iraq, and Lebanon. Saudi Arabia is one of the most important centers of Sunni Islam, while Iran is the primary homeland of Shia Muslims. The agreement committed both the Saudis and Iran to a path of renewed mutual diplomatic engagement and, as Wang Yi put it, "strengthening communication and dialogue" and "realizing good neighborliness and friendship." Both countries also agreed that the development of their economies and the promotion of improved livelihoods for their people should be their priorities. Officials in both Teheran and Riyadh remarked that they welcomed China's role as a mediator, which was a great contrast to the United States' destructive interventions in Iraq, Afghanistan, Syria, and Libya.

Over many years, China has persistently and strongly advocated for the rights of the Palestinian people. When Israel unleashed its genocidal war on Gaza following the Al-Aqsa Flood in October 2023, China immediately called for a ceasefire, an end to the occupation of Palestinian lands, and reiterated its support for a Palestinian state, which would be admitted to the United Nations. As with the agreement forged between Iran and Saudi Arabia, China sought to resolve differences between the various political groups active in Palestine, most particularly Hamas and al-Fatah. In July 2024, as Israel's campaign of death and destruction in Gaza raged on, fourteen different organizations met in Beijing for discussions mediated by

Foreign Minister Wang Yi. On July 23, they announced that they had agreed to set aside their differences and commit themselves to working together to establish a unified Palestinian government when Israel ceases its attacks in Gaza and the Occupied Territories. Once again, China was able to play this mediating role and bring together previously irreconcilable parties to reduce tensions and promote a future of peace and development, though the Palestinian people face tremendous challenges even once the fighting will have come to a halt. Three days after the signing of this agreement, which came to be known as the Beijing Declaration, the war criminal Israeli Prime Minister Benjamin Netanyahu received a standing ovation from the US Congress, was fawned over by President "Genocide Joe" Biden at the White House, and feted by the fascist ex-president and felon Donald Trump in Florida.

The first years of the 2020s also saw China pursuing diplomatic initiatives in the Pacific Ocean region, as well as in its complex relationships with the European Union and various European states. In the Pacific, China extended economic aid, investments, and other assistance programs to several island nations, including the Solomon Islands and Vanuatu. Some of this was through the Belt and Road Initiative, while other projects were bilateral agreements for specific development activities. The United States had been used to viewing the Pacific Ocean as an "American lake," especially since the end of World War II, but in recent decades had largely ignored the region. Unsurprisingly, US media and politicians were quick to denounce Chinese investment and aid to Pacific Island countries as interference in a US sphere of influence and as destabilizing the established world order. Australia, which often functions simply as a local vassal of US imperialism, also expressed its opposition to Chinese assistance to developing peoples across the Pacific region. Australia's relationship with China has been self-contradictory over many years. Trade between China and Australia has grown steadily, with China buying large quantities of grain and investing in major mining operations in the country, but Australian politicians have generally continued to see their primary allegiance as that to the US. A deal with the United States in September 2021 to provide nuclear submarines was an effort to cement Australia's links as a subordinate component of the project to contain and threaten China. Since, Australian naval vessels have also taken part in US-incited provocations in the South China Sea. China has sought to maintain good relations with Australia on the basis of the principles of mutual respect and mutual benefit, even in the context of these activities.

Europe has been a particularly complex arena for China diplomatically. While a number of European states are participating in the Belt and Road Initiative, including Italy, Hungary, Serbia, the Czech Republic, Lithuania, the Slovak Republic, Latvia, and Poland, the degree of their engagement has varied considerably. The European Union is China's largest trading partner in both imports and exports. But since 2019, the EU has characterized China as a "systemic rival" and relations have been increasingly strained. NATO, the US-dominated military group to which most European states belong, has adopted a steadily more hostile attitude towards China, though the People's Republic poses no military threat to Europe whatsoever. Under pressure from the US, NATO has even been reaching out to Asian countries like Japan and South Korea to promote anti-China activities. US propaganda promoting the idea that China plans to "invade" Taiwan has been used to try to draw European countries into dangerous and reckless involvement in its program of containment and possibly into a US-provoked war with China.

The two most important relationships between China and Europe have been with Germany and France, the two largest members of the EU and NATO. The recent course of these relations has been one of significant contrast. Germany accounts for the largest share of China's trade with Europe, with the automobile industry holding particular importance. From 2005 to 2021, German Chancellor Angela Merkel made seven visits to China on trade missions during her time in office. Nonetheless since 2020, Germany has been more and more critical of China. It has joined in the United States' efforts to inhibit China's development through embargoes on high-tech equipment, and through banning Chinese 5G technology from German markets. France's relations with China have been somewhat more consistent. While France has joined in the criticisms of China promoted by US propaganda, it has refrained from complete subordination to US dictates. President Emmanuel Macron, while hardly a progressive force in domestic politics, has argued that France should reduce its dependence on the United States, emphasizing that it should not allow itself to be drawn into any confrontation between China and the US over Taiwan or other issues. He has also spoken in favor of efforts to reduce the central role of the US dollar in world trade, in line with China's efforts to promote new global financial infrastructure.

As China celebrated the seventy-fifth anniversary of the founding of the People's Republic on October 1, 2024, it found itself in a complex and challenging international situation. The management of relations with an increasingly reckless, hostile, and dysfunctional United States was a top priority, but efforts to build new infrastructures, both material and institutional, to free itself and other developing countries from US imperialist domination were also advancing across much of the world. China could look back on the history of the PRC as one in which it went through clear phases of development, which shaped its relations with the wider world.

In the first three decades after liberation, China had struggled to find a path forward in the construction of a socialist economy and society. In this era, China sought to promote revolutionary activities in many countries in Africa, Asia, and Latin America. From the end of the 1970s through the first decade of the twenty-first century, China embarked on the program of reform and opening, during which, in order to most effectively acquire the investments, technologies, and other inputs from the global capitalist system, it adopted a low-profile posture in international affairs. This was the age of accommodation with the United States and the capitalist core, the years of biding time and building capabilities. China curtailed its support of revolutionary movements, and even aligned much of its foreign policy actions with those of the United States.

With the world financial crisis of 2008, which broke out in the United States and spread throughout much of the global economy, China began to enter a new era. China's socialist system allowed the country to weather the storm of the crisis with relatively little damage. The new era, in which we still remain, emerged fully with the United States' Pivot to Asia in 2011 and the election of Xi Jinping and Le Keqiang as leaders of the Communist Party of China and the government of the People's Republic in 2012. The dozen years of this new era have seen China shed its deference to the United States and chart a new course in its relations with the rest of the world. A more confident China has undertaken great initiatives to transform both its own economy and that of developing countries around the world, including the Belt and Road Initiative, the Asian Infrastructure Investment Bank, and BRICS. China has lifted hundreds of millions of its people out of poverty, saved millions of lives during the COVID-19 pandemic, and become the world leader in alternative energy. For people in poor and developing countries around the world, China's socialist system, which is still a work in progress, has become an inspiration in their own efforts to build better futures for themselves. Throughout the history of the PRC, the Five Principles of Peaceful Coexistence, based on mutual respect, mutual benefit, guaranteeing the sovereignty and territorial integrity of all states, and noninterference in the internal affairs of any country, have been the foundation of relations between China and the world.

BIBLIOGRAPHY

Brautigam, Deborah. *The Dragon's Gift: The Real Story of China in Africa*. Oxford, UK: Oxford University Press, 2009.

This is an excellent study of China's activities in Africa, including investments, aid projects, and development loans. Brautigam refutes the various claims of neocolonialism or exploitative extraction levelled against China with facts and figures based on years of fieldwork. She has written several books since this one, further updating her research, but this remains a classic statement of the realities of China's engagement with the continent.

Chen Jian. *Zhou Enlai: A Life*. Cambridge, MA: Harvard University Press, 2024.

Chen Jian has written a massively detailed study of the life of Zhou Enlai, based both on extensive archival research and on interviews with a wide range of sources in China and elsewhere. This is a tremendously valuable resource for the study of Zhou's life and of the political affairs in which he was involved. It is filled with detailed information about China's foreign policy and activities, and presents accounts of important debates and decisions about relations with the Soviet Union, the United States, India, and many other aspects of China's relations with the rest of the world. It is deeply marred by Chen's bizarre portrayal of the relationship between Zhou and Mao Zedong, who is presented in a simplistic caricature as a manipulative, power-hungry, almost apolitical individual. One must read past

Chen's anti-Mao hysterics to get the most out of the useful material which abounds in this volume.

Curtis, Simon, and Ian Klaus. *The Belt and Road City: Geopolitics, Urbanization, and China's Search for a New International Order.* New Haven: Yale University Press, 2024.

Curtis and Klaus go beyond the usual studies of the Belt and Road Initiative to consider how the infrastructure developments being advanced through the BRI are producing new urban environments that constitute nodes within an emerging multicentric global system no longer dominated by US imperialism. This is not a work of Marxist scholarship, but is nonetheless valuable as a study of the actual contributions China is making to improving the lives of hundreds of millions of people all over the planet. More than half of the human population now lives in cities, and China's programs of investment and development are shaping the future of urban life in new ways seeking a "future of shared prosperity for all."

Freymann, Eyck. *One Belt One Road: China's Power Meets the World.* Cambridge, MA: Harvard University Asia Center, 2021.

Despite its ridiculous cover showing Xi Jinping in imperial robes, this is a serious study of the BRI, refuting many of the bourgeois claims of neo-imperialism or debt-trap diplomacy. Freymann sets out case studies of BRI projects in South Asia, Africa, and Europe to show how China is working with poorer and developing countries to create new infrastructure and productive capacities. China's relations with BRI countries are based on the idea of mutual benefit, which means that both China and the host country benefit, but not in an exploitive, extractive way. BRI is not a philanthropic practice, but it is a win-win arena for all concerned.

Gardner, Kyle J. *The Frontier Complex: Geopolitics and the Making of the India–China Border, 1846–1962.* Cambridge, UK: Cambridge University Press, 2021.

China's relationship with postcolonial India has been complex and volatile, with the dispute over the border between the two countries exemplifying the sometimes contentious, sometimes cooperative engagement between them. Gardner's book shows how the ambiguities of border delineation arise from the colonialist program of territorial definition, carried out by the British from the mid-nineteenth century, and inherited by India with independence in 1947. Coping with the legacies of colonialism has been a fundamental component of China's relations with countries in Asia, Africa, and Latin America. This book shows how deep the roots of contemporary problems in postcolonial nations can be.

Lewis, John Wilson, and Xue Litai. *China Builds the Bomb*. Stanford: Stanford University Press, 1988.

When the Soviet Union withdrew its aid and experts from China at the end of the 1950s, one of the most critical areas of concern for the Chinese leadership was the program to develop their own atomic weapons. In the context of US threats to use atom bombs in the Quemoy Crisis in 1958 or against the Viet Minh during the First Indochina War in the early 1950s, China had relied on the Soviets for a nuclear umbrella of protection, but in the wake of the Sino-Soviet split it became critical for China to have its own atomic capabilities. Lewis and Xue tell the story of how China successfully pursued its objectives and developed the ability to deter US aggression and the threat of a nuclear attack by building its own bomb and testing it in October 1964.

Li Danhui and Xia Yafeng. *Mao and the Sino-Soviet Split, 1959–1973: A New History*. Lanham, MD: Lexington Books, 2020.

Li and Xia make extensive use of Chinese archives and interviews with Chinese officials to present a reasonably straightforward history of the Sino-Soviet Split. This episode is so important that it is worthwhile engaging with their scholarship, even when published by a press whose ancestry goes back to CIA infiltration of academic publishing in the 1950s.

Li Minqi. *The Rise of China and the Demise of the Capitalist World Economy*. New York: Monthly Review Press, 2008.

Li Minqi presents a vision of how China's economic development and its increasing engagement in global economic relations will indeed be disruptive of the long-established dominance of the West. China's reemergence as a significant power and the socialist nature of its reform-driven growth will create alternative opportunities for production, distribution, and consumption, no longer as a matter of the endless accumulation of profit for the capitalist elite, but as social accumulation providing the capacity to address basic human needs and create a better, sustainable future for humanity.

Mao Tsetung (Zedong). *A Critique of Soviet Economics*. New York: Monthly Review Press, 1977.

Understanding the dynamics of Sino-Soviet relations, which were at the heart of China's overall international position in the 1950s and 1960s, must be grounded in understanding the political perspective of Mao Zedong and much of the Chinese leadership, and how it developed over the decades. Mao's critique of the ways in which the Soviet experience of economic development had distorted the socialist system in the USSR and led to the alienation of the Soviet Communist Party from the masses underpinned much of the domestic political conflicts of the first three decades of the People's Republic. This text presents Mao's analysis and outlines how his perception of the Soviet model shaped his fears and objectives in China, including how China should relate to both the capitalist world dominated by the United States and the revolutionary struggles taking place in Asia, Africa, and Latin America. This perspective is critical for an understanding of the Sino-Soviet Split.

McGuire, Elizabeth. *Red at Heart: How Chinese Communists Fell in Love with the Russian Revolution*. Oxford, UK: Oxford University Press, 2018.

The Soviet Union was a source of inspiration during the years of revolutionary struggle in China, and after liberation became China's "big brother" in the first decade of building socialism. McGuire's book is a study how ordinary people in China formed personal connections with the Soviets, including close friendships and professional collaborations from the 1920s to the end of the 1950s, and considers how the rupture between China and the USSR affected these relationships.

Schaller, Michael. *The United States and China: Into the Twenty-First Century*. Oxford, UK: Oxford University Press, 2016.

Schaller is a mainstream bourgeois political scientist, and this work is framed in the rhetoric of power politics. Nonetheless it provides a comprehensive overview of US policies and actions concerning China from the nineteenth to the early twenty-first century. China's shifting perceptions and analyses of US imperialism were not always in line with what the United States was up to, and Schaller's study sets out the other side of the story. The long-term objectives of US expansion in the Pacific and its efforts to retain hegemony globally are clearly delineated in this book.

Shen Zhihua and Xia Yafeng. *Mao and the Sino-Soviet Partnership, 1945–1959*. Lanham, MD: Lexington Books, 2017.

As with the study of the Sino-Soviet Split by Xia Yafeng and Li Danhui cited above, this book draws on otherwise generally difficult to access archives and sources in order to present the history of the decade and a half of close engagement between China and the Soviet Union. The tremendous contributions made by the Soviets, both in terms of state and party relations and on the more personal level of encounters and collaborations between Soviet advisors and their Chinese counterparts, should never be overlooked or marginalized.

Weber, Isabella M. *How China Escaped Shock Therapy: The Market Reform Debate*. New York: Routledge, 2021.

As China embarked upon the course of reform and opening in the 1980s, there were sustained and lively debates about how far to go and how fast to go there, what the nature of reform should be, and how to preserve the socialist system while making the best use of market mechanisms. The program of reform was both a major reorientation of domestic policies and a profound endeavor of engagement with global capitalism and the United States in particular. Weber's book is by far the best discussion and analysis of the debates of the early to mid-eighties and reveals the dialectical relationship between China's past and present, as well as the unprecedented effort to chart a viable course of socialist construction without succumbing to the anarchy of the marketplace. The contrasting experience of the Soviet Union and the socialist states of Eastern Europe make this study even more relevant and valuable.

Zhao Suisheng. *The Dragon Roars Back: Transformational Leaders and Dynamics of Chinese Foreign Policy.* Stanford: Stanford University Press, 2023.

Zhao Suisheng presents a classic political science/international relations study of China's foreign policies and international conduct under the leadership of Mao Zedong, Deng Xiaoping, and Xi Jinping. Despite this focus on "great men" and a general disregard for the social and political developments taking place in China since 1949, this book contains a good deal of valuable and useful information if read with a suitably critical eye.

www.ingramcontent.com/pod-product-compliance
Lightning Source LLC
Chambersburg PA
CBHW031427120626
46545CB00006B/2307